THE KNOWLEDGE CREATION POTENTIAL
OF MANAGEMENT CONSULTING

The Knowledge Creation Potential of Management Consulting

Francesco Ciampi

Florence University, Florence, Italy

IOS Press

Amsterdam • Berlin • Oxford • Tokyo • Washington, DC

© 2008 The author and IOS Press.

All rights reserved. No part of this book may be reproduced, stored in a retrieval system,
or transmitted, in any form or by any means, without prior written permission from the publisher.

ISBN 978-1-58603-870-0
Library of Congress Control Number: 2008927761

Publisher
IOS Press
Nieuwe Hemweg 6B
1013 BG Amsterdam
Netherlands
fax: +31 20 687 0019
e-mail: order@iospress.nl

Distributor in the UK and Ireland
Gazelle Books Services Ltd.
White Cross Mills
Hightown
Lancaster LA1 4XS
United Kingdom
fax: +44 1524 63232
e-mail: sales@gazellebooks.co.uk

Distributor in the USA and Canada
IOS Press, Inc.
4502 Rachael Manor Drive
Fairfax, VA 22032
USA
fax: +1 703 323 3668
e-mail: iosbooks@iospress.com

LEGAL NOTICE

The publisher is not responsible for the use which might be made of the following information.

PRINTED IN THE NETHERLANDS

Contents

Introduction   vii

Chapter One
The Changing Roles of Management Consultants   3

Chapter Two
Knowing through Consulting in Action:
a Challenging and Unexplored Field of Research   15

Chapter Three
Defining Management Consulting   25

Chapter Four
The Diachronic Interpretation: the Consulting Process   43
    1. Setting Up the Consulting Relationship   44
    2. Diagnosing the Entrepreneurial Problem   50
    3. Planning the Therapy   56
    4. Implementing the Solution   61
    5. Evaluating Results and Concluding the Process   65

Chapter Five
The Synchronic Interpretation: the Consulting Models   73

Chapter Six
The Cognitive Interpretation: Meta-Consulting
Knowledge Creation Pathways   87
    1. Nonaka and Takeuchi's Organizational
       Knowledge Conversion Spiral   87
    2. Meta-consulting Knowledge Conversion Pathways   91

References   103

Introduction

The literature offers a wide selection of studies into enterprise knowledge management (Abrahamson, 1996) and management consulting (Whittle, 2006). Management consulting firms are often discussed as being the archetypes of knowledge-intensive firms (e.g., Alvesson, 1995; Crucini, 2002; Heller, 2002; Werr, 2002), or as the firms whose core product is knowledge itself (Sarvary, 1999). Consulting firms are generally aware of the value of knowledge for their own organizations and for their clients[1]. However, the subject of knowledge creation potential that can be activated through the concrete implementation of management consulting interventions still remains a largely unexplored research area. This book interprets management consulting from a knowledge perspective, and proposes a general conceptual framework for investigating and interpreting that potential.

In Chapter One, I outline the main dynamics of change that characterize today's demand for management consulting, and suggest that firms are becoming increasingly aware of the real cognitive (rather than only the economic) value generation potential that can be activated through the consulting relationship.

---

[1] The increasing awareness among consultancies of the knowledge creation potential of management consulting is confirmed, for example, by the progressive and empirically detectable change in the range of management consulting services offered and their modes of delivery: creating and sharing knowledge (in terms of exploration, development and exploitation) have now become key-channels for transferring value to clients (Davenport & Prusak, 2005). Moreover, many of the top consultancies now "offer knowledge management services for their clients, focusing on how they can develop their internal knowledge management practices" (Buono and Poulfelt, 2005, p. IX).

I also look at the possible pathways for evolutionary transformation of consulting practices, models and roles that consulting firms could follow if they want to take advantage of the important changes that are taking place.

In Chapter Three, I propose a definition of management consulting which aims to identify the distinctive ontological (real, essential and relatively stable) features of this particular service and emphasizes the mainly cognitive nature of its value-creation potential. I go on to discuss two approaches to interpreting management consulting: the diachronic approach (the consulting process), and the synchronic approach (the consulting models). I use these approaches to outline the essential variables of the consulting relational dynamics.

In Chapter Six, I make use of the theories interpreting knowledge creation processes as knowledge conversion processes (Nonaka & Takeuchi, 1995), and apply them to the specific context of management consulting relationships. This allows me to propose a possible framework of the cognitive pathways along which knowledge can be created through management consulting. It highlights the fact that in "meta-" (i.e., advanced) consultancy contexts the knowledge creation potential of consulting lies in the possibility that it can generate not only explicit knowledge but also (even, mainly) new tacit entrepreneurial knowledge, such as new interpretative abilities (vision of the firm's structure and of the competitive environment), new experience-based diagnostic skills, and new capabilities to gain insights into solving entrepreneurial problems. The value of this knowledge for both the client and consultant goes far beyond the solution of the specific problem for which the consultant was engaged.

The aim is not to demonstrate the absolute validity of this model, but more simply to highlight its internal theoretical consistency and to discuss the supporting evidence of a number of anecdotal cases[2], which are used to better clarify the conceptual

---

[2] The brief empirical evidences provided in this book are based on interviews by a group of researchers who are exploring (under my guidance) the

framework, rather than serving as empirical evidence for the validity of the model[3].

Testing the validity of the proposed framework through a systematic quantitative analysis is the next challenge I intend to undertake. Another challenge is to develop management control tools which can translate the conceptual model into practice, into systems that can support management consulting firms and their clients in the consulting relationship knowledge management.

Perhaps a better understanding of the knowledge creation paths that can be activated by management consulting projects following the meta-consulting approach will allow both clients and consulting firms to increase their awareness of the entrepreneurial knowledge generation potential engrained in the dynamics of the consulting relationship. Clients and consultants might be better placed to consciously define knowledge creation goals for their consulting projects, to effectively design and manage the related cooperative learning dynamics, and to evaluate the cognitive value (rather than only the economic value) of the consulting intervention results. Client firms might come to regard the management consultant's work not simply as "seeking a solution to a specific problem" but also as "facilitating the endogenous development of their cognitive capacities" (and hence of their distinctive capabilities). They could then select the consultant and, above all, plan their active cooperation in the consulting process on this basis. Similarly, consultants may be encouraged to interpret the consulting relationship as an opportunity for cooperative learning. This may not only increase the client's cognitive resources, but also enable consulting firms

---

emerging issues in knowledge management within the context of the European management consulting industry. This research project is being conducted with two samples of firms; one comprising fifty management consultancies of various sizes, and the other with over one hundred large and medium-sized corporations. The interviews are still in progress and will be completed by the end of 2008.

[3] This approach is frequent in management literature. See, for example, Normann (2001).

to develop new and unique knowledge (which only the specific consulting context can induce), and, consequently, new distinctive consulting capabilities that may be fundamental for their competitive success.

The proposed conceptual model may have two major limitations. First, it may be subject to the limitations that some authors (e.g., Gourlay & Nurse, 2005) attribute to Nonaka and Takeuchi's theory of organizational knowledge[4]. The second, and more important, limitation is that the individual knowledge creation pathways and the whole conceptual framework from which they stem still need to be more thoroughly investigated, so as to test their interpretation potential in diverse consulting settings (in terms of the consulting firm's size, structure and sector/specializations, and in terms of the client firm's size, structure and industry, for example).

---

[4] To my mind, however, Nonaka and Takeuchi's organizational knowledge creation theory does still remain a very powerful tool for interpreting knowledge creation entrepreneurial processes.

Chapter One

The Changing Roles of Management Consultants*

Frequent environmental discontinuity[1] and intense changes in the competitive dynamics and logics of client business areas[2] are transforming the physiology of the management consulting industry. This turmoil is generating uncertainty about the direction of the future structural evolution of the industry, but may also present interesting development opportunities for consulting companies with proactive attitudes toward change.

---

* See Ciampi (in press-a).

[1] For example: the "dot.com bubble" which burst in the first months of 2000 (with consequent restructuring and downsizing of numerous sectors of the telecom industry), and the tragic events of September 11th, had considerable impact on levels of activity (and therefore, turnover) and the economic results achieved in several sectors of the consulting industry; then there was the collapse of Enron that not only brought about the disappearance of one of the "Big Five" (Arthur Anderson), but had also extremely negative effects on many consulting and auditing firms; the recent bursting of the subprime mortgage bubble has had a considerable negative impact over past months on rating and financial consulting firms.

[2] The following represent some of the principal competitive dynamics that characterize the majority of industries in the developed economies: the globalization of markets and companies; the shortening of product life cycles and of "time to market"; growing competitive pressure in domestic markets and a resulting exponential increase of resources to be invested in activities such as new product development, renovation of old products, exploration and penetration of emerging markets; fierce cost competition by manufacturers located in emerging markets; and the exponential development of Information Technologies. These emerging competitive issues are all having a strong impact on the strategies and the organizational structures of most of the client companies served by the main management consulting firms, whether they are big or small, local or international, generalist or specialized.

The consulting business is, despite everything, still growing. According to Kennedy Information's 2007 annual survey on the global consulting market, the aggregate turnover in this industry reached about 285 billion dollars in 2006 (with an increase of 10% from 2005) and in the next four years it is expected to see an annual growth rate of higher than 7% (aggregate turnover is expected to reach 375 billion dollars in 2010)[3].

Meanwhile, the complexity and the articulation of the consulting demand is also growing. The value chain of client firms is being reconfigured. On the one hand, both material activities (e.g., the production and assembly of components) and low-value added immaterial ones (e.g., the management of technological infrastructure, and back office activities) are being increasingly outsourced. On the other hand, knowledge-intensive activities (hard to imitate and reproduce), such as product and process R&D, customer service, the creation, development, and protection of critical strategic and organizational knowledge and competences, are being increasingly internalized.

The client firm's tendency to internalize intellectual activities (intellectual in-sourcing[4]), such as strategic planning, competitive analysis, human resources selection and development, and marketing planning impacts on the consulting industry boundaries; and it also makes the needs of the client evolve. Intellectual in-sourcing enhances the client firm's capability to consciously select, design, and control the value-creation dynamics which

---

[3] One interesting analysis of the management consulting industry was carried out by Toppin & Czerniawska (2005). One explanation for the development of management consulting (based on transaction cost theory) has been given by Canback (1998; 1999).

[4] If knowledge is becoming *the* resource on which the entrepreneurial organizations operating in developed economies base their competitive advantages (and their strategic development processes) it should not come as a surprise that this should be seen as "the challenge" to be faced in the years to come by management consulting firms, being as they are the "archetypes of knowledge-intensive firms".

can be activated through the consulting relationship[5]. This internalization tendency consequently acts as a strong stimulus for management consulting firms to go beyond their traditional intervention models[6].

The economy is now in large part globalized, and founded on the widespread use of modern Information and Telecommunications Technologies. Today's "market-space" competition (that is "...competition completely unconstrained by physical geographical boundaries..." where "...space becomes a competition factor..." in itself), at the appropriate time ("time-based competition") and of the immaterial ("...dominated by intangible supply features and by virtual spatial coordinates...") is turning the competitive logics and dynamics of the firm upside down (Brondoni, 2002a; 2002b; 2007). Traditional strategic reactions (temporary

---

[5] More and more frequently the top and middle management positions of many medium to large client firms are held by former senior consultants of major consulting firms (and/or by graduates of international business schools that offer the most updated training in "best management practices"), who are well able to master the consulting techniques and models used by top consultancies. Consequently, the control and development of the "cutting edge" strategic and organizational analysis techniques and models are no longer the exclusive competence of the leading consulting firms.

[6] Such models see the members of consulting teams as "experts", possessors of "superior" knowledge, management tools and implementation skills, whose simple "transfer" would enable clients to achieve "certain" results in terms of attaining/strengthening their competitive advantage. BCG has traditionally founded its competitive strategies on the "unique" abilities of its consultants in the application of the "growth share matrix" and the "experience curve model". Monitor founds its competitive strategies on its "higher" interpretive capabilities in the "value-chain model"; Strategos on its analysis and enhancement skills of the "core competencies", etc. (Poulfelt, Greiner, & Bhambri, 2005). However, with increasing frequency many of the abstract conclusions and recommendations of the consulting firms (not only those made by "generalist" consulting firms or by firms specialized in the strategy field but, even if on a smaller scale, also those made by firms specialized in sectors traditionally considered to be "at a high level of standardization", such as credit rating firms and accounting auditing firms) reveal growing implementation issues and/or, when tested against the reality of hard facts, lead to results which are very far from what had been promised.

downsizing, restructuring, outsourcing, consolidations by means of mergers and acquisitions, etc.) may turn out to be inadequate.

Whether or not consulting firms will successfully compete in the market will depend in large part on their capacity to undertake new and diverse strategic pathways, which will change their business boundaries, their organizational profiles, and many features of the consulting practices and the consulting models that have traditionally been the basis of their competitive success.

We already have some examples of proactive strategic behaviors toward environmental change, such as:

- the diversification of services offered: outsourcing providing is added to traditional consulting activities. Nowadays a considerable amount of the turnover of some of the major consulting firms (among others IBM, Accenture, and Deloitte Consulting) comes from the direct management of activities that their clients have decided to outsource (from supplier management, to IT infrastructure management, to routine human resources management, to back office management);
- the development of networks and alliances with both internal and external players in the consultancy industry, thus progressively overcoming the traditional model of "stand alone" consulting firms. This development path was initially undertaken by the IT consultancies (think of the alliances between Accenture and Hewlett-Packard, between SAP and numerous IT consultancies) and I think we will see it progressively spread among the more "proactive" players of other sectors of the industry. The imperatives of globalization are leading an increasing number of consulting firms (specialist or generalist) to consider strategic partnerships, especially with different sized players and with consultancies operating in different geographical markets. For small consulting firms, alliances with bigger and internationalized companies mean that they will be able to assist clients in the planning and implementation of their international development proc-

esses. For large consulting firms, small consulting boutiques that operate on a national or regional basis can be ideal partners for alliances aimed at achieving service adaptation/personalization (to cultural and competitive local contexts) for both traditional clients (big and medium-sized firms that are implementing strategic paths of redefinition of their value chains and markets for a global and, therefore, multi-localized base), and for new clients that are a natural target of their international development (typically medium-sized firms with high growth potential and bases in emerging markets)[7];
- the orientation toward long term consulting relationships that exceed implementation times of a single project. It is estimated that nowadays more than two thirds of the annual turnover of consulting firms in leadership positions in the various sectors of the industry originate from clients they had already acquired in previous years (Poulfelt, Greiner, & Bhambri, 2005). One of the advantages of this type of relationship is that there are lower marketing costs and lower investments (also for the client). And it is easier and cheaper to build and maintain the client's trust and the consulting firm's credibility.

Figures 1 and 2 are an attempt to systematize and project present-day dynamics, where demand is increasingly aware of the real economic and cognitive value generation potential that can be activated by the consulting relationship. The figures show two possible scenarios of the evolutionary transformation of management consultant's roles.

In those consulting areas characterized by "low knowledge creation potential", typically IT consulting and consulting on routine functional area related problems (accounting consult-

---

[7] Today the turnover growth rates of many top consultancies are much higher in the emerging markets than in the traditional ones (Europe and USA). For instance, in 2007 Deloitte global network's growth rate in Asia reached 17,2%, almost 50% higher than that achieved in the USA (11,9%).

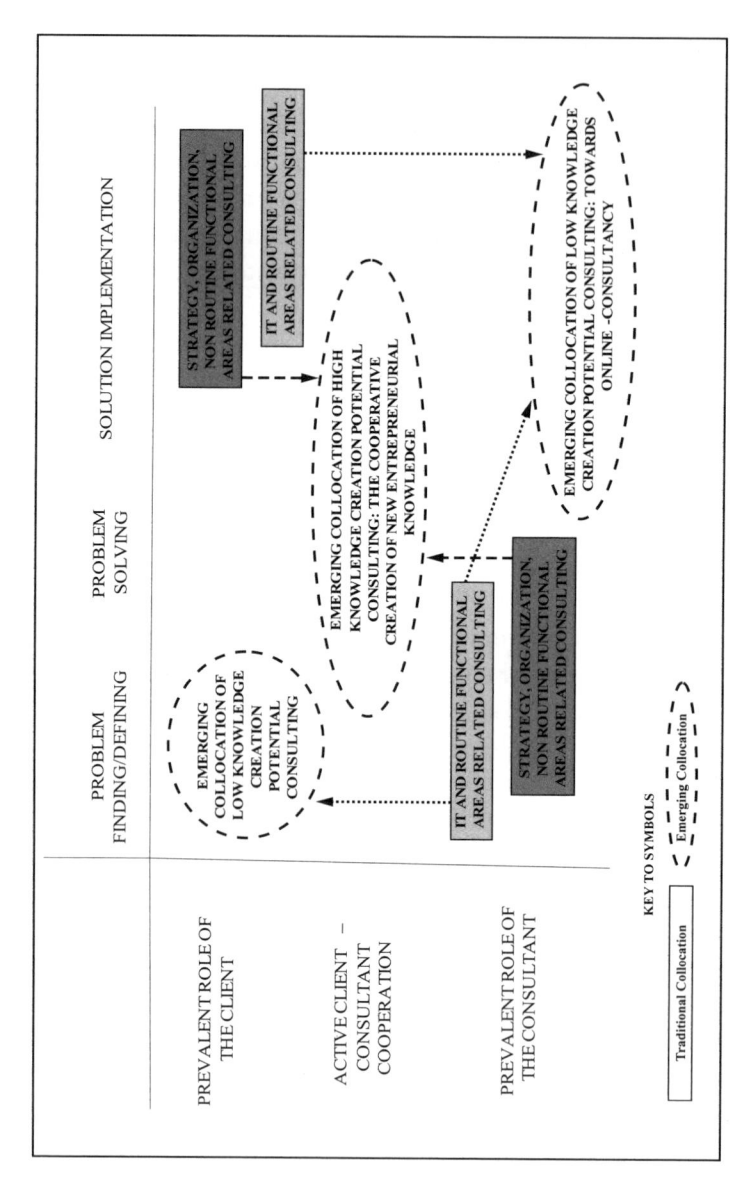

Figure 1. Emerging issues in the management consulting relationship: increasing cooperation and personalization (- - →) vs. increasing separation and standardization (······▶).

ing, auditing consulting, etc.), the pressure from the demand is for standardization and cost reduction in low-value added activities (operations management, IT infrastructure management and low knowledge-intensive immaterial activities). This is generating the need for the client firms to further delegate problem solving and implementation activities to consultants, and to focus company time and attention on aspects of problem finding and problem defining (e.g., which activities should be standardized, and with which cost reduction objectives), and on control of the consulting project (intermediate and final) key results.

Such a scenario leads us to think that a possible evolution of the management consultant's role could be toward:

- the "online-consultant". This limits face to face interactions with the client to a bare minimum, incorporates diagnostic and problem solving best practices into modular software, and delivers consulting services through extensive use of the internet and/or of dedicated intranet platforms (Czerniawska, 2005). The use of ICT platforms will also satisfy the growing need of clients to be able to obtain quick and simple access to full control of progress made in the implementation of the consulting intervention; and/or
- the "outsourcing provider", which tends to take on the management of those activities that client firms decide to outsource (a decision that might be based on advice given by consultants themselves).

A different evolutionary path is predictable for the role of management consultants operating in areas characterized by "high knowledge creation potential" (typically: strategy consulting, organizational consulting, consulting on non-routine functional area related problems). In this respect, the growing propensity of client firms to internalize activities characterized by greater knowledge intensity (intellectual in-sourcing) and, consequently, to more consciously evaluate the real effectiveness of any consultancy intervention is progressively leading these firms to prefer management consulting models characterized by:

- greater involvement of consultants in the concrete implementation of change management solutions, and compensation criteria for consulting services founded on concrete, achieved results ("success fees");
- greater involvement of the client in phases traditionally delegated to the consultant (problem finding, diagnosis, solution discovery). The progressive "reappropriation" of the problem defining and solutions specification phases will allow the client firm to more promptly verify the effectiveness of the consulting intervention, to benefit from a more customized service, to exploit its own pre-existing diagnostic capabilities (no one knows the specific entrepreneurial setting with which the consulting intervention has to deal better than the client). Above all, client firms will be able to maximize the development opportunities of new and autonomous knowledge and capabilities that will allow them to successfully manage future entrepreneurial problems, which may not necessarily be similar to those that were object of the consulting intervention.

Therefore, in consulting areas characterized by "high knowledge creation potential" the competitive power of the management consulting firm will also depend on its capacity to overcome traditional service logics (geared to the simple transfer to the client of mainly explicit knowledge -"best practices"-, in order to resolve specific entrepreneurial problems), and to evolve its consulting practices toward models[8] designed to provide support, collaboration and facilitation for the creation of new, mainly implicit knowledge (managerial skills, change management abilities) that enhances the cognitive resources of the client firm and its capability to successfully face future strategic challenges. In this respect we should, however, notice that:

---

[8] On the consulting models see Chapter Five.

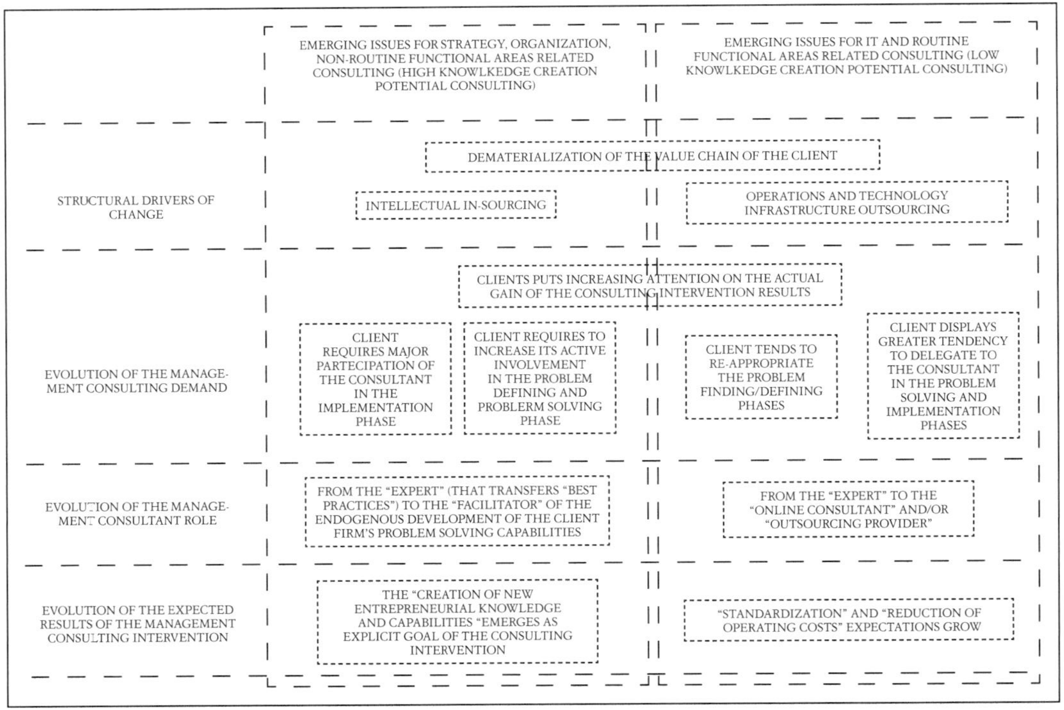

Figure 2. Emerging management consultant roles: "Facilitator" of new entrepreneurial knowledge and capabilities creation processes vs. "Online-Consultant" and/or "Outsourcing Provider".

1. notwithstanding the official claims of some consulting firms[9], the empirical evidence (e.g., Linnarsson & Werr, 2002) shows that even today the (economic and, above all, cognitive) value-creation opportunities related to the transition from consulting approaches geared to the transfer of "best practices" (consultant as expert) to consulting approaches geared to the cooperative creation of new knowledge and entrepreneurial capabilities (consultant as a facilitator of new entrepreneurial knowledge and capabilities creation processes) are rarely consciously perceived and, consequently, are not adequately planned for and exploited;
2. despite the vast amount of international literature on enterprise knowledge management and management consulting and despite the fact that management consulting firms are often referred to as the archetypes of knowledge-intensive firms, the subject of knowledge creation potential that can be activated through the concrete implementation of management consulting interventions still remains a largely unexplored research area. This will be discussed in the next Chapter.

---

[9] In the communications to the market made by the big consultancies that offer "high knowledge creation potential" consulting services, we may often notice such claims as "Our clients outperform the market 3 to 1" (Bain), or "We are successful if our clients have built in-house capabilities to solve their own problems the next time around" (McKinsey). See Poulfelt, Greiner, & Bhambri (2005, p. 14).

Chapter Two

Knowing through Consulting in Action: a Challenging and Unexplored Field of Research·

Knowledge is the main resource for underpinning the strategic development processes of entrepreneurial organizations (e.g., Drucker, 1995; Grant, 1996a)[1]. Knowledge Management (KM) has consequently become a key theme both in management literature and in corporate practice (Abrahamson, 1996)[2]. Traditional KM literature interprets knowledge as something that people own (the *knowledge-as-possession* view), which has an essentially explicit nature and that is relatively easy to transfer (e.g., McElroy, 2000; Ruggles, 1998). Hence traditional KM literature mainly

---

· On this topic see Ciampi (in press-b).

[1] Knowledge, human resources, and (intra- and inter-organizational) social relationships all now have higher levels of competitive value, as assets, than more traditional resources such as capital and natural resources. In addition to the interesting and original ideas put forward by Rullani (1994; 2004a; 2004b) and Vicari (Vicari & Troilo, 1999), for a general overview of these themes see, for example, OECD (1999) and the studies conducted by Bettiol (2005), Berini & Guida (2000), Cohen & Low (2002), Cravera, Maglione, & Ruggeri (2001), Davenport & Prusak (1998; 2000), Eppler (2003), Lipparini (1998; 2002), Michaud & Thoenig (2004), Panzarani (2004), Prahalad & Hamel (1990), Rifkin (2000), and Stewart (2002). Regarding "intellectual capital" (which has gained popularity as a theme in economic and management literature only in the last decade), I should like to pay tribute to the older, but in no way less original studies, conducted by Becker (1962; 1964; 1976) and Schultz (1958; 1960; 1962; 1981).

[2] There are many and often heterogeneous contributions in the literature on knowledge management and on learning organizations. On the wide debate of these themes see, for example, Daft (2001) and Garvin (1998). For some Italian experiences of enterprise knowledge management, see Genova & Montironi (2004) and Minguzzi (2006).

focuses on techniques for gathering, imitating and disseminating knowledge - in essence, transferring the best practices (Newell, 2005). Conversely, the most recent literature (the *knowing-in-action* view) interprets knowledge as being mainly tacit, socially constructed, embedded in practice, context-dependent (Johnson, Marakas, & Palmer, 2000), difficult to transfer (Szulansky, 1996), and therefore really valuable only when it is generated in a specific reference context (from which the *knowing-in-action* metaphor stems), thus shifting the focus of analysis from transferring only the best practices to creating and maintaining ideal conditions in order to fully realize the knowledge generation process potential (Blacker, 1995; Buono & Kerber, 2005)[3].

As far as it contributes to solving entrepreneurial problems, consulting either disseminates or creates knowledge. It disseminates by applying already adopted solutions and practices to problems and needs that are new for the client. It directly creates knowledge by proposing solutions for problems that are new to the world or that become new in the presence of events which are external to the client.

Such a basic distinction is corroborated by the international literature specifically concerned with management consulting. Without delving into the vast literature on practical consulting techniques, offering recipes on how to consult (e.g., Armstrong, 1993; Bellman, 1990; Block, 2000; Freedman, 2000; Schaffer, 1997a), how to start (e.g., Biech, 1998; Biech & Swindling, 2000), to manage (e.g., Maister, 1993), to protect (e.g., Shenson, 1990a) and to develop (e.g., Bly, 1998; Lambert, 1997; Shenson, 1994; Shenson & Wilson, 1993; Weiss, 1992) a consulting practice (Kass & Weidner, 2002), an analysis of the main literature enables one to identify two main interpretative paradigms of the management consulting relationship.

---

[3] It is however only on the development of new interpretative paradigms, able to join "…the pole of codified knowledge…" and "…the pole of contextual knowledge…" (Rullani, 1994, p. 68), that an economic theory which is really able to explain "…when and why knowledge is produced, exchanged and used in the economic circuit" (Ibid., p. 48) can be founded. See also Rullani (2004a, 2004b).

The first approach interprets the role of the consultant as a problem-solver and/or a supplier of expert knowledge (the *expert consultant* approach). According to this interpretative model, the firm engages the services of a consultant because it is facing some difficulties and/or is sensing symptoms of dysfunction, and entrusts the consultant with the responsibility of conducting a diagnosis (problem finding) and, subsequently, identifying and suggesting a solution (problem solving). The *expert consultant* must be endowed with specialized skills consistent with the specific (business and industry) sector of the consulting intervention, including those needed to tailor possible solutions to the client's particular setting (Bessant & Rush, 1995; Greiner & Metzger, 1983). Under the *expert consultant* approach, the knowledge creation potential of the consulting relationship is limited (almost ignored as far as the client's role is concerned), and the knowledge which is transferred travels primarily in the consultant⇒client direction, taking on a mainly codified character.

Under the second interpretative approach (the *process-consulting* approach), the client retains full ownership of the problem in every phase of the consulting process, while the consultant acts as a guide in the diagnostic activity (which nevertheless mostly remains the client's responsibility) as well as a facilitator in the solution discovery and application phases (Schein, 1987; 1988; 1999; Stjernberg & Werr, 2001). Starting from its initial phase, the intervention aims to fuel and develop the client firm's self-diagnosis and problem-solving capabilities, by setting in motion a bidirectional (consultant⇔client) transfer of mainly *process* (and hence tacit) knowledge. The *process-consulting* model has a far greater cognitive potential, and both parties in the relationship play a critical role in it, even though the knowledge creation potential connected with the use and the conversion of the consultant's explicit knowledge appears to be underestimated (Linnarsson & Werr, 2002).

To better understand the way consulting induces knowledge creation, it is however necessary to investigate the real cognitive dynamics through which the consulting relationship is implemented.

However, in neither of the aforementioned literature streams are there any specific, thorough analyses aimed at examining the cognitive paths through which new entrepreneurial knowledge creation is (or can be) induced by concretely implementing the consulting relationship.

The same limitation can also be found in the more recent literature which has adopted a specifically cognitive perspective in investigating management consulting (Buono, 2002; Clark & Fincham, 2002; Engwall & Kipping, 2002a; Engwall & Sahlin-Andersson, 2002a). Among the issues examined in this literature are:

1. management consultants acting as mere "filters" for the growing volume of knowledge produced outside the firm (Ernst & Kieser, 2002) or management consultants as "information brokers/knowledge arbitrageurs" (Semadeni, 2001);
2. management consultants acting as "management knowledge carriers and disseminators" within the "management knowledge industry" in general (e.g., Bessant & Rush, 1995; Fridenson, 1994; Kipping & Armbrüster, 2000) and, more specifically, as knowledge disseminators throughout the EU of the "best management practices" (see Alvarez, 1998b; Engwall & Kipping, 2002a; Engwall & Kipping, 2002b; Engwall & Sahlin-Andersson, 2002b)[4];
3. the internal KM procedures and systems of management consulting firms (e.g., Anand, Gardner, & Morris,

---

[4] Of the diverse research projects that aim to study the creation and dissemination of the "best management practices" throughout Europe, special mention should be made of the CEMP program (The Creation of European Management Practice), sponsored by the European Union. "The CEMP programme had three objectives: (1) to judge to what extent education, research and consulting are contributing to a homogenization in European business practice; (2) to determine whether this homogenization is more developed in some parts of Europe than in others; and (3) to contribute to an improvement of the European dimension in the diffusion and consumption of management knowledge" (Engwall, Alvarez, Amdam, & Kipping, 2001, p. 5).

2007; Bou & Sauquet, 2005; Bukh & Mouritsen, 2005; Haas & Hansen, 2005; Henriksen, 2005; Stjernberg & Werr, 2003);
4. limitations to and risks connected with the use of codified KM systems founded on the wide spread use of Information and Communication Technologies, due to the inability of ICTs to manage the uncodified (implicit) part of the knowledge that is created and transferred (Dunford, 2000; Kim & Trimi, 2007; Reihlen & Ringberg, 2006);
5. the problems involved in integrating KM systems in consulting firm mergers and acquisitions (Ejenäs & Werr, 2005; Gammelgaard, Husted, & Michailova, 2005);
6. management consulting firms' knowledge strategies: exploring new consulting practices *vs.* exploiting already known consulting practices (Baaij, Van den Bosch, & Volberda, 2005a);
7. the mechanisms through which professional institutions affect knowledge creation in professional service firms (Robertson, Scarbrough, & Swan, 2003);
8. the relationships between knowledge strategies and organizational structures in professional service companies (Empson & Morris, 1998);
9. the learning potential related to the realization of strategic alliances between management consulting firms (Chung, Luo, & Wagner, 2006).

Only a small number of recent studies have shed light on the importance of the knowledge creation dynamics involved in the concrete implementation of management consulting interventions. Some authors have focused their attention on the complexity of the knowledge creation processes involved in the adaptation of the consultant's codified knowledge to the client's specific setting and the building among them of "communities of practices" (Todorova, 2004); on the importance of client-consultant face-to-face interaction to professional service firms' knowledge development processes (Fosstenløkken, Løwendahl, & Revang, 2003); on the mainly tacit and socially constructed nature of knowledge created and used in consulting interventions (Newell, 2005; Visscher, 2006); on the factors which enhance, or reduce, the effectiveness of consultant-to-client knowledge transfer processes (Kirsch, Ko, & King, 2005; Lahti & Beyerlein, 2000); and on the role of "epistemic communities" (Cowan, David, & Foray, 2000) and "communities of practices" (Lave & Wenger, 1991) in interpreting and evaluating the impact of the management consulting intervention on the knowledge structure of the organization where the intervention takes place (Creplet, Dupouet, Kerna, Mehmanpazir, & Munier, 2001). Others have highlighted the dynamic and (tacit and explicit) composite nature of the knowledge that is used/generated in consultancy activities as a consequence of the fact that in order to discover solutions, consultants must have the ability to apply pre-existing explicit knowledge to the specific consultancy context on a case-by-case basis (thus converting explicit knowledge into new tacit knowledge) as well as (and above all) "the ability to relate to the specific situation without having a...normological model". Thus "the consultant, through processes of reflection and analysis, tends to become [also] a researcher" (Jensen, 2005, pp. 372-374), that is to say, someone who is able to produce knowledge through insight as well as through externalization (i.e., conversion into new explicit knowledge) of experience-based (and hence, tacit) knowledge[5].

---

[5] I believe that an important contribution to the evolution of management sciences could be achieved by leaving the narrow confines of traditional academic views of research and consulting, whereby the main role of research is to create new knowledge, and the main role of consulting is to apply existing knowledge to concrete corporate contexts (Bonnet, Moore, Savall, & Zardet, 2001). Management researchers need to be able to scientifically observe the object studied (the firm) and firms are increasingly complex, heterogeneous, and changeable. I am firmly convinced that observing the researched object "form inside" and adopting an "intervention view" makes our observations much more comprehensive than if we only observe the firm from outside. Our results and contributions to the development of management sciences could be far more significant if researchers were willing (and able) to act as consultants, even only for research purposes ("intervener-researchers"). The "scientific consultancy" approach has had excellent results in France, for

Even though these recent studies have highlighted the potential fecundity of investigating the "in action" management consulting knowledge creation dynamics, they never do delve deeply into those dynamics and, consequently, "our understanding of what actually happens with consultant knowledge (in essence their main product) and the knowledge of the client organization …[still remains]… murky at best" (Todorova, 2004, p. 74).

example, at the Institut de Socio-Economie des Entreprises et des ORganisations (ISEOR). This is discussed in Buono & Savall (2007) and in Bonnet, Moore, Savall, & Zardet (2001). Perhaps it is useful to recall that as early as 1977, after the 1976 conference they had hosted on management consulting, the Academy of Management approved the following "Position Statement on Professor/Consultants": "The Academy of Management is supportive of professional consulting activities by its members when these activities are conducive to the professional growth of the individual and contribute to the management discipline through the enrichment of teaching, research, and understanding of the field" (Gore & Wright, 1979, p. 34).

Chapter Three

Defining Management Consulting

Numerous definitions of management consulting have been proposed in the literature (e.g., Barcus & Wilkinson, 1995; EIU, 1993; Greiner & Metzger, 1983; Kass & Weidner, 2002; Kubr, 2002; Salvemini, 1987; Steele, 1975)[1].

---

[1] The literature has a wide range of possible definitions for management consulting, which have been proposed by scholars and management consultants. The following are examples and not intended to be a comprehensive list:
- Kubr (2002, p. XXI) defines management consulting as a professional service that helps managers to analyze and solve practical problems, and transfers successful management practices from one enterprise to another;
- the UK Institute of Management Consultants (EIU, 1993, p. 16) defines the management consulting service as "a professional service" provided by "an independent and qualified person …. to business, public and other undertakings by: 1) identifying and investigating problems concerned with strategy, policy, markets, organisation, procedures and methods; 2) formulating recommendations for appropriate action by factual investigation and analysis with due regard for broader management and business implications; 3) discussing and agreeing with the client the most appropriate course of action; 4) providing assistance where required by the client to implement his recommendations";
- Salvemini (1987, p. 46) defines consultancy as "…a series of services aiming to identify and solve enterprise decision problems, with a specific type of clientele (executives and managers) …";
- Steele (1975, p. 3) defines management consulting as "any form of providing help on the content, process, or structure of tasks or series of tasks, where the consultant is not actually responsible for doing the task itself but is helping those who are";
- Greiner and Metzger (1983, p. 7) state that "Management consulting is an advisory service contracted for and provided to organizations by specially trained and qualified persons who assist, in an objective and independent manner, the client organization to identify management

The conceptual delimitation of management consulting proposed here is an attempt to identify the distinctive ontological (real, essential and relatively stable) features that qualify the inner nature of this particular and fascinating service activity (Ciampi, in press-b; in press-c).

I define management consulting as a *service activity performed by persons that are external to, and independent from, the client and that possess appropriate scientific-professional skills and abilities, and consisting of providing opinions in order to enable the client to identify and solve entrepreneurial problems that involve top management functions, using a rectifying, progressive and/or creative approach, and thereby contributing to the creation of new entrepreneurial knowledge* (see Figure 3).

1. *The independence of the consultant.* Consultants must be able to express their assessments and opinions objectively and impartially (e.g., Kubr, 2002) without being influenced by other purposes than those inherent in solving the entrepreneurial problem for which the assignment was given[2], whether these "other purposes" coincide or conflict with those of the client firm's teleological structure[3], or are complementary to it.

---

problems, analyze such problems, recommend solutions to these problems, and help, when requested, in the implementation of solutions".

The diverse definitions can be grouped as follows, depending on the interpretative approach adopted (Kubr, 2002):
 a. those with a functional approach ("management consulting as a method");
 b. those that interpret management consulting as a specific type of professional service ("management consulting as a profession").

[2] One of the consultant's main responsibilities is to assist client firms in defining the entrepreneurial problem from their viewpoint and in such a way as to protect their interests (Schaffer, 1997a; 1997b; Turner, 1982). The consultant must withstand any opportunistic temptations (Ormerod, 1997) to pursue other purposes (Saxton, 1995), such as inducing the client to purchase what the consulting firm wants to sell, rather than what the client really needs (Madigan & O'Shea, 1997).

[3] The firm's basic teleological system, elaborated systemically by Carlo Vallini (1991), consists of the following main categories of purposes:

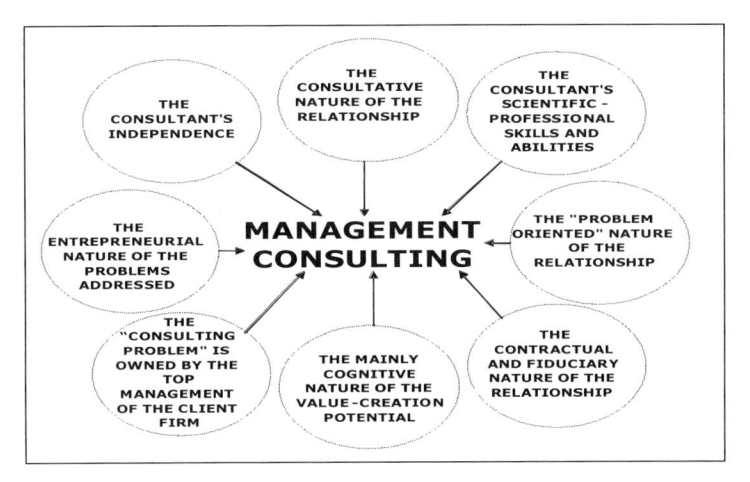

Figure 3. Distinctive ontological (real, essential and relatively stable) features of management consulting: a synthetic conceptual framework.

From this, it follows that consultants must be independent in financial terms (they must have no direct or indirect financial

    a. *motivational* purposes, i.e. relating to the two systems on which the firm's foundation and development are based (ownership system and top management system);
    b. *end-goal* purposes (i.e. relating to clients). A firm can only exist, and grow, if it is able to satisfy the needs of a body of clients who wish to buy and consume/use the goods or services that the firm provides;
    c. *instrumental* purposes, directly connected to the diverse types of resources required in the firm's operational processes. This category includes purposes relating to:
      i) the firm's employees; and
      ii) the firm's suppliers of material, financial or information resources;
    d. *autogenous* purposes, relating to the firm as a whole. They can be summed up as a natural tendency to grow, quantitatively (in terms of capital investment, turnover, number of employees, market share, etc.) and qualitatively (in terms of technological innovation, product innovation, organizational innovation, etc.);
    e. *constraint* goals, i.e. the goals connected to the social environment in which the firm operates, and which may "impose" constraints on the firm's business operations (by way of legal norms), and/or induce constraints non-coercively (company ethics), so as to safeguard the community's quality of life.

interests regarding the client firm), in decision-making terms (there must be no client-consultant relationship of super- or sub-ordination), and in emotional terms (there must be no psychological influences that might impair the consultant's necessary "emotional detachment"). The consultant's independence in all these quarters will enable him/her to adopt cognitive and behavioral approaches consistent with the fiduciary remit given by the client[4].

2. *The scientific-professional skills required of the consultant.* Management consultants must be able to guarantee an effective and independent approach by virtue of their possession of (and capacity to use) appropriate scientific-professional skills and abilities (e.g., Frankenhuis, 1977; Kellogg, 1984; Madigan & O'Shea, 1997; Terno & Young, 1986), acquired through specific training[5] and/or previous entrepreneurial and/or consulting experiences, and recognized by the other members of the professional com-

---

[4] Following the financial scandals (Enron in the US, Parmalat in Italy, etc.), involving numerous national and international consulting firms, both the academic world and the consulting firms have focused major attention on the issue of the management consultant's independence and ethical behavior (see Hagenmeyer, 2007). This has reopened a wide debate on the motivations that move (or should move) companies to employ management consulting firms (e.g., Buono, 2002; Cambell, 2002; Czerniawska, 2002a). On the ethical issues involved in intervening in client organizations, see (for example) Ozley & Armenakis (2000). Maula & Poulfelt (2002) present an interesting critical analysis of the Codes of Conduct and the Ethical Codes compiled by international management consulting associations. They highlight the fact that "the majority of the Codes tend to support one-directional, i.e. 'directive', 'content-based', and 'transplantation-based' types of consulting. In the cases where the Codes recommend interaction, they could emphasize two-directionality and mutual interaction between the consultant and the client more clearly and explicitly, in the spirit of 'non-directive', 'process-based' and 'translation-based' consulting models" (Maula & Poulfelt, 2002, p. 1).

[5] On the setting up of "corporate universities" by management consulting firms (i.e., a department specifically for the training of their human resources), and on the features such "internal" centers should have, see Nevins (1998).

munity[6]. This feature is emphasized by the definitional approach which interprets *management consulting as a profession*[7], therefore identifying its essence precisely in the particular professional skills and expertise[8] owned by the consultant[9].

This aspect of the consulting activity is obviously important in every phase of the consulting process, even though it sometimes appears not to be adequately taken into account by consultancy firms. The following comments were made by the chief executive officer of Studio Roscini S.p.a. (an Italian garment design company whose clients include numerous leading international companies in the fashion industry, such as Gucci, Fendi, Valentino and Tod's) regarding the conduct of a consultancy firm he

---

[6] This does not mean that management consulting is a profession in the formal sense of the word. A comment made by Dean (1938, p. 455), that "Profession is used in literature in discussing management consultants for lack of a more accurately descriptive term" is in some ways still valid today. In the course of the last decade, both the literature and the "real consulting world" have become increasingly attracted by the idea of setting up official professional bodies and/or registers to certify (and therefore render formally recognizable) the professional requirements for management consultants. Whether or not it is opportune for consulting firms to achieve full professional status (in view of the role these firms played in the collapse and crises of a number of big American firms), is discussed by McKenna (2006). Groß & Kieser (2006, p. 1) believe that "professionalization efforts among consultants … will never be successful if the classical concept of professionalism is applied".

[7] This approach emphasizes the professional qualities that management consultants should have (specific capabilities, qualifications and knowledge) and those to be required of the service (complexity, discretion, etc.).

[8] In this connection, *professional discretion* is paramount, since it guarantees that client information will not be used outside the consulting relationship. So is the specific competence required in terms of skills and knowledge for client problem-solving (*present professional qualities*), and the ability to keep on developing competence by studying theories and by learning new business and consulting practices (*potential professional qualities*). Consultancy should act as a connection between business theory and practice, between the academic world and the practical world of the firm (Kubr, 2002).

[9] Greiner and Metzger's 1983 definition belongs to this approach. It is cited in Note 1.

had commissioned to design and implement a new Enterprise Resource Planning (ERP) system.

> A partner and two senior managers of the consultancy firm attended the first two meetings. These meetings were so productive we had already defined the project goals and the timing even before formally entering into the consulting contract. But after engaging that firm we only met junior managers and trainees and all these people, even though technically skilled, never gave us the impression they were up to the task. The project was a failure, and we were forced to go back to our old ERP system. I am certain that if the project had been followed up by the two senior managers we had met the first time, things would have worked out differently.

3. *The consultative nature of the client-consultant relationship.* Management consulting consists of providing opinions, not advice, for advice would be a deviation from the requirements of objectivity and independence (including emotional independence) which should always characterize the consultant's work. Management consulting sets into motion a process of collaborative information and knowledge exchange between the consultant, whose responsibility concerns the quality and objectivity of the opinions provided, and the client, who is ultimately responsible for applying or rejecting the opinions received. The following comments were made by the chairman of a major Italian bank regarding the work of a consulting firm engaged for the development of a new internal credit rating system.

> The consulting firm demonstrated that the new rating model worked better than the one we had previously used (as it enabled us to evaluate our customers' credit rating much better), and this model is now effectively underpinning our credit policies. However, none of us was involved in all the phases of designing the model, and as a result, none of us is fully aware of the mathematical and statistical rationale underlying the way it operates and the complex weighting criteria used for the several variables it utilizes: the model is simply like a "black box" as far as we are concerned. How will we be able to improve that model in the future? And above all, how can we change it if it eventually turns out not to be reliable in the future (in

a changed economic situation, with a different qualitative composition of our client base, etc.)?

The consultative nature of the relationship is emphasized by the definitional approaches which interpret *consulting as a method*, therefore finding its essence in its consultative function to the client when making decisions and/or performing certain tasks (e.g., Cohen, 1989; Steele, 1975).

4. *The "problem-oriented" nature of the relationship.* Management consulting consists of identifying and defining problems (diagnosis), working out solutions (therapy), and subsequently applying those solutions (cure)[10]. The problem-oriented nature of management consulting[11] makes it all the more necessary to establish an appropriate level of cooperation between the consultant and the client[12] in each phase of the consulting process.

---

[10] Excluding the solution implementation stage from the consulting process, on the grounds that the consultant's role is advisory and it is the client who must implement the solution (Fleming, 1989), does not, to my mind, take into full consideration the question of the consultant's responsibilities. It is true that clients are responsible for deciding whether or not to adopt proposed solutions, and also for deciding how implementation should be carried out, just as they are responsible for choosing which consultant to hire. However, it is equally true that consultants cannot refuse some reasonable responsibility for the effectiveness of their opinions, by simply saying "it is not their job" to implement the solution, since it is this stage that puts those opinions into practice and "to the test against the reality of hard facts".

[11] Since management consultants act as problem solvers, their main function is often defined in the literature as "reducing the uncertainty" with which the client firm's senior managers have to cope (e.g., Ernst & Kieser, 2002; Lundberg, 2002).

[12] Regarding the need for client and consultant to take equally active (and equally important) shares in the consulting process, and to set up an informal process of "give and take" between equals, see Lippitt & Lippitt (1986). On the need for there to be close collaboration between client and consultant if the organizational changes are to be realized effectively, see (for example) Fischer & Rabaut (1992), Gelinas & James (1998) and Katcher (1972).

Here is what I was told by the managing director of the Italian division of a pharmaceutical multinational.

> We are accustomed to dealing with (and seeking to solve) problems all the time (often many problems at one and the same time). We often have to make rapid decisions regarding prioritizing the different problems. We can decide to set aside some of them in order to solve the most urgent ones, but we cannot evade problems or pretend not to see them. I can immediately recognize people who are endowed with problem-solving skills and attitudes, and when I have to choose a consultant (whatever the task might be) these are the skills and attitudes I look for.

To be effective as problem solvers, consultants need a wide range of skills, such as analytical skills, synthetic skills, and creative skills, and, if the intervention model adopted is of the meta-consultancy type[13], maieutic and empathetic skills are also required. For each skill, there is a minimum threshold value below which it is unlikely that the consulting intervention will be successful[14].

5. *The contractual and fiduciary nature of the management consulting relationship.* The remit is given by the client firm and accepted by the consultant in the form of a contract, which may be succinct or detailed, and will not necessarily always be written down, through which both parties agree to confer full legal and psychological legitimacy to the consultancy activity. Among the underlying elements of the consultancy relationship, originating with the negotiations carried out in the initial phase of the consulting process, are the formal and clear definition of the consulting intervention goals (Armenakis & Burdg, 1988; Ford, 1985; Kellogg, 1984; Kolb & Frohman, 1970; Shenson, 1990b; Turner, 1982), the rights, duties and roles of each party involved

---

[13] See Chapter Five.

[14] For more general considerations on the strategic capabilities that are critical for the success of management consulting firms, see Kumar, Simon, & Kimberley (2000).

(legal contract), and their conscious commitment to cooperate in a climate of mutual trust (Czerniawska, 2006a; 2007; Galford, Green, & Maister, 2000a; 2000b; Green, 2006) and respect[15] (psychological agreement).

> The most difficult thing during the initial phases of contact with a new potential client is understanding whether I can trust him (whether he is sincere, whether he is really interested in the expertise I can offer, etc.) and above all, convincing him that he can trust me. Experience has taught me that being totally transparent can create a sense of insecurity in the other party (I have "lost" many potential clients for this very reason), but in the long term it certainly pays off: in the remits I have been given in the past 10 years I have always received the maximum cooperation from my clients, and only in one case have I been criticized for not fully attaining the consultancy project goals (and in our profession attaining 100% of the objectives within the given timescale is the exception, rather than the rule).

These are the words of a founding partner of an Italian medium-sized strategic consulting firm.

6. *The entrepreneurial nature of the problems addressed.* Management consultants address entrepreneurial problems (strategic, organizational and/or related to one or more specific functional areas) whose solution can significantly affect the structure of the client firm[16] (whether small or large, manufacturing or services,

---

[15] In addition to there being a relationship of mutual respect and trust between the client firm and the consulting firm, it is of course equally necessary that there be a good working atmosphere among the members of the consulting team who will carry out the intervention. On this subject, see (for example) Maister & McKenna (2002a). For a wider discussion of human resources management in management consulting firms, see Maister & McKenna (2002b).

[16] When I refer to *the firm's structure*, I have in mind a simplified representation that aims to give a global picture of the firm's system, by identifying the *essential* and *relatively stable* morphological features of the ownership structure, the management structure and the operating system. This representation can be obtained by inductively identifying the features in the firm which are:

etc.), generate changes in its state[17], set in motion development, stabilization or turnaround strategic processes[18] (Ciampi, 2004; Fazzi 1982, 1984), and ultimately have innovative effects[19], supported by evolutionary changes in knowledge (rationalizing change rationales), attitudes (acceptance and internalization of motivations for change), individual and group behavior (concrete actions to bring about change); in one word: changes in corporate

- *essential*, because they are especially significant and differentiate the firm from all other firms;
- *relatively stable*, because they tend to be constant in modality and/or level and are subject to change only through important environmental turmoil or deliberated management decisions.

If we look closely, the firm's structure is the link between a descriptive analysis of the firm and an interpretative analysis of its change processes. It is both the result of the top management's decisions and the object upon which the management acts. The qualitative and quantitative features that make up the firm's structure can only be specified through a "subjective" simplification process undertaken by the members of the top management and influenced by these members' personalities, and by the main structural features of the firm's competitive environment. See Fazzi (1982; 1984) and Ciampi (2004) in this connection.

[17] Regarding the definition of the "substance of entrepreneurial problems" as being "gaps" between the actual, present state of the firm's structure, or its realistically foreseeable state, and the ideal (sought-for) state of this structure, see Section 2 in Chapter Four.

[18] In terms of top management decision-taking, the strategic process can be described as an induced change in the firm's structure (decided by the top management), which can be quantitative and/or qualitative and is designed to increase the strategic strength of the firm. The *development strategic process* is a radical, positive change in the firm's structure and is designed to reach new levels of strategic strength. In the *stabilization strategic process*, the aim is to maintain and defend already achieved levels (stabilizing its structure allows the firm to consolidate advances made during periods of development). In the *turnaround strategic process*, the aim is to return to prior levels which have been lost during a period of crisis. In physiological conditions, the firm's life can be seen as a succession of development and stabilization processes. For further detail, see Fazzi (1982; 1984) and Ciampi (2004).

[19] Concerning the innovative effect generated by strategic processes, see Vallini (1991). On the importance of the innovating function of management consulting, see Greiner & Metzger (1983).

culture[20] (Kubr, 2002). Over the last two decades, the scope of the entrepreneurial problems addressed by management consultants has gradually expanded to cover the whole gamut of a firm's management activities[21]. Some authors maintain that identifying

---

[20] It is vital that the consultant be able to take steps to remove/reduce the "resistance to change". The degree of resistance may vary; but there is nearly always some form of resistance, especially in the solution implementation stage. For further considerations, see Sections 2 and 4, in Chapter Four, and also Chapter Six.

[21] A framework of the typical management consulting intervention areas could prove useful toward building a full picture of management consulting activities.

Consultants can make use of a wide range of methods, tools and techniques, in order to solve management problems concerning the following management decision areas:

   a. strategy (strategic diagnosis and strategic planning techniques, industry analysis techniques, value chain analysis techniques, business planning techniques, etc.);
   b. organization (macrostructure (re)projecting techniques, microstructure (re)projecting techniques, management style diagnosis/evaluation/development techniques, competence diagnosis/evaluation/development techniques, etc.);
   c. finance (financial restructuring techniques, facilitated credit access techniques, etc.);
   d. production (techniques for diagnosing and (re)projecting production cycles, techniques for diagnosing and (re)projecting stock management policies, techniques for (re)projecting quality control policies, etc.);
   e. marketing (techniques for diagnosing and (re)projecting sales promotion policies, techniques for diagnosing and (re)projecting pricing policies, techniques for diagnosing and (re)projecting distribution policies, market research methods, etc.);
   f. human resources (techniques for finding and selecting managerial staff, techniques for coaching, training and developing managerial staff, techniques for (re)organizing managerial career structures, etc.);
   g. IT systems (e.g., techniques for diagnosing and (re)projecting IT management control systems);
   h. administration (techniques for optimizing tax policies, techniques for optimizing balance sheet and budgeting policies, etc.);
   i. R&D (techniques for strategic R&D orientation, techniques for new product and new process development management, etc.).

the management consultant's "specialized areas of expertise"[22] lies at the heart of defining the management consulting concept: a list can be compiled of certain specialized fields of expertise,

Each consulting intervention assignment is normally given to solve problems that are mainly located in one management decision area. However, given the systemic nature of entrepreneurial decisions, and problems, the intervention will almost certainly need to deal with aspects belonging to one or more of the other areas.

[22] There are many classifications of the management consultant's intervention areas. Table 1 shows that proposed by the European Federation of Management Consulting Association.

Table 1. The management consultant's intervention areas (FEACO, 2005).

Corporate Strategy Services	Strategic Planning/Organisation Development
	Mergers & Acquisition
	Market & Competitive Intelligence
	Sales/Marketing/Corporate Communications
	Financial Advisory
Operations Management	Business Process Re-engineering
	Change Management
	Customer/Supplier Relation Management
	Project Management
	Turnaround/Cost Reduction
	Purchasing & Supply Management
Human Resources Management	HR Strategy & HR Marketing
	Executive Coaching
	Recruitment/Search & Selection
	Benefits, Compensation & Retirement
	Performance Measurement & Management
	Training & Development
	Talent Strategies
Inf. Tech.	IT Consulting
	IT System Development & Integration
Outsourcing Services	

Czerniawska & May (2006) and Greiner & Poulfelt (2005) give interesting overviews of emerging trends in the main management consulting sectors.

and it is assumed that whoever supplies services in those specific fields may be defined as a management consultant. I do not share this view since, not only does it fail to bring out the essential features of management consulting, but it also generates obsolete definitions because of the changes to which the consulting intervention spheres are constantly subjected (Aiello, 1996; Clark & Fincham, 2002).

7. *The entrepreneurial problem that is the object of the consulting intervention ("the consulting problem") concerns the client firm's top management.* The problems to be faced by the management consultant (directly or indirectly) concern the functions of the client firm's senior managers which are "not delegable" (Ciampi, 2004; Fazzi, 1982) and, consequently, the consulting problem must (directly or indirectly) regard at least one person belonging to the client firm's top management (which therefore represents "the primary client"[23] of the consultant).

> I immediately decided to take up the KPMG offer, even though the starting salary they proposed was 20% lower than what I was paid by Alfa Consulting[24] [a company offering Information and Communication Technologies services to manufacturing firms]. Even though I had become a senior manager, our consultancy projects almost invariably dealt with the technical aspects of the client's technological infrastructure and my interlocutor was always an EDP employee and/or an employee of an external company, to which our client had outsourced the maintenance of its technological facilities. I was not working for an ICT management consulting firm, but for a company offering IT infrastructure maintenance services.

This statement was made by one of the candidates that KPMG Italia recruited in 2006, after a lengthy selection process.

8. *The mainly cognitive nature of management consulting value-creation potential.* The creation of new knowledge and the de-

---

[23] See Chapter Four, Note 8 on the definition of "primary client".

[24] Some of the firms mentioned in this book wished to remain anonymous, and I have therefore used invented names for these firms.

velopment of new entrepreneurial (diagnostic, therapeutic and/or interpretative) skills and capabilities, which both the client firm and the consultant can exploit once the consulting project has been completed, are the most significant potential results of the management consulting intervention[25]. However, empirical evidence shows that, despite the official claims of some consulting firms[26], it is extremely rare for this potential to be consciously perceived and fully exploited. There are, in fact, very few cases where the client and the consultant consciously set knowledge creation goals for the consultancy project (Linnarsson & Werr, 2002). Furthermore, their efforts are very often taken up entirely by merely replacing the client's existing practices with the "best practices" (mainly explicit knowledge) which the consultant proposes to "transfer" to the client (e.g., Ernst & Keiser, 2002; Newell, 2005). By so doing, both parties in the consultancy relationship renounce contextualizing the best practices proposed by the consultant in relation to the specific client firm environment. They renounce socializing their pre-existing implicit knowledge base, and they also renounce embarking upon new practices and knowledge social construction pathways (Lave & Wenger, 1991). However, not only does implicit knowledge often constitute the most valuable cognitive resource owned by both parties, but it

---

[25] I consequently find myself in disagreement with contributions in the literature (e.g., Abrahamson, 1996; Abrahamson & Fairchild, 1999; Clark & Salaman, 1998b; Madigan & O'Shea, 1997; Shapiro, 1996) that take a "skeptical approach" and view management consulting firms as "systems of persuasion creating compelling images which persuade clients of their quality and work" (Clark & Salaman, 1998b, p. 18), and management consulting as an activity that does not produce value for client firms but detracts value, and that leads to relationships that are always very heavily weighted in the management consulting firm's favor. On the relationship between management fashions and management consulting, see the interesting contribution by Williams (2004). On the opportunity to be open-minded and flexible, and to base one's judgment on the specific consulting context, when interpreting the consulting relationship and the "power" relationships among those involved, see Fincham (1999a) and Sturdy (2002).

[26] See Chapter One, Note 9 in this connection.

also represents the main potential outcome of the consulting intervention. From this it follows that even in cases where the consultancy intervention is deemed successful (because it has made it possible to solve the problem the consultant had been commissioned to solve), a big part (often the most important part) of the potential cognitive value of the relationship is often lost and/or not adequately exploited. I will address this specific feature of consultancy activity in greater depth in the final Chapter.

Figure 4 provides a synoptic overview of the distinctive ontological (real, essential and relatively stable) features and logical relations which, according to my proposed definition, qualify the essence of management consulting activity.

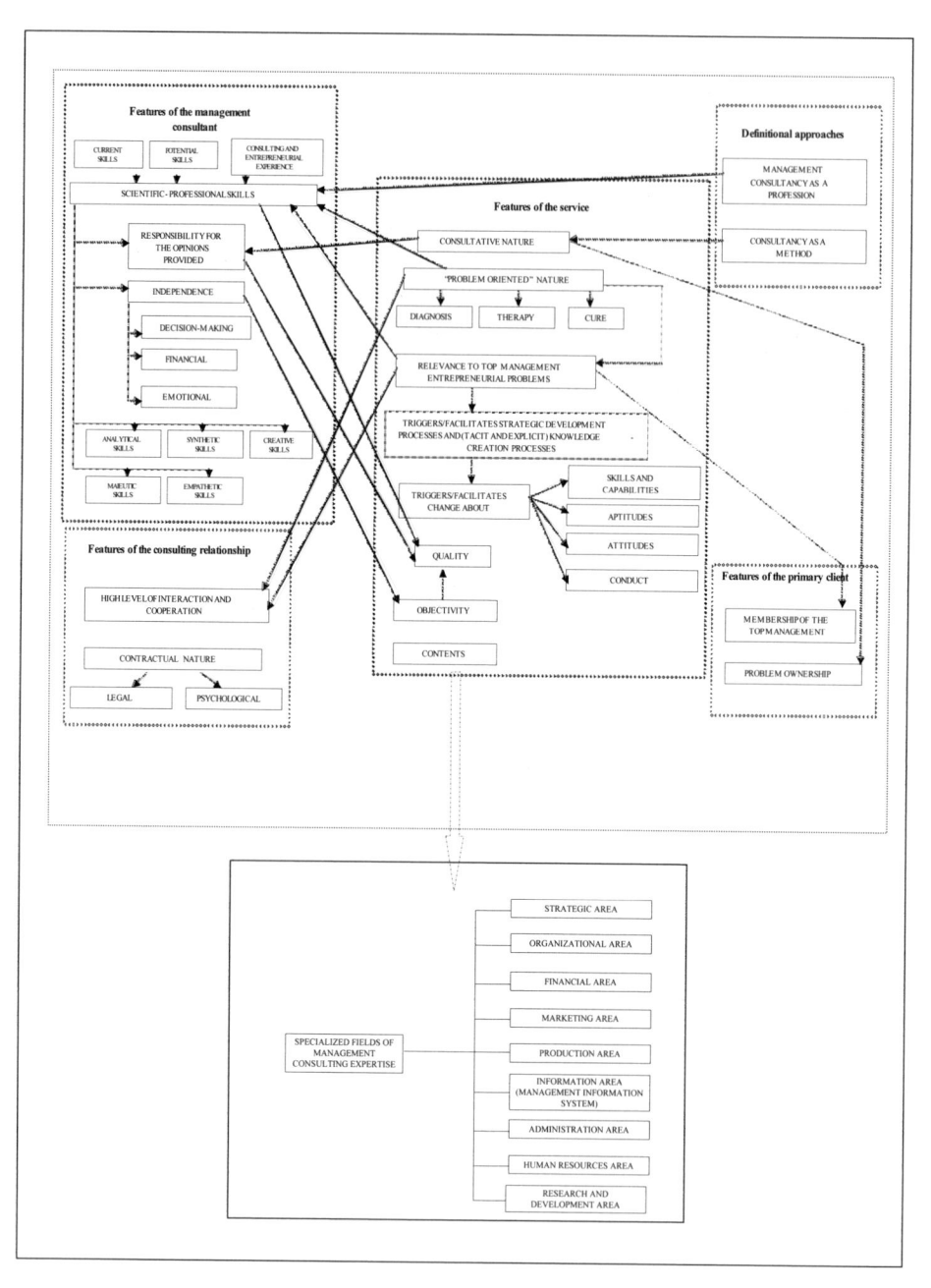

Figure 4. The ontology of management consulting activity: features and logical relationships.

Chapter Four

The Diachronic Interpretation: the Consulting Process

Figure 5 provides a schematic presentation of the different stages in the process[1] of management consulting[2].

In real contexts, this process tends to take place with varying degrees of reiteration, and completeness[3], and it is also physiological for the different phases to develop "along parallel lines", instead of sequentially. In this Chapter, for each stage, I shall examine the main contents (work to be done), the specific elements of risk and criticality, and the ensuing aptitudes and skills required of the consultant[4] (and also of the client) for the phase to be carried through successfully.

---

[1] In the literature, the consulting intervention is often seen as a *process* with a number of sequential stages. My interpretation of the consulting process draws mainly on the studies by Kubr (2002) and Greiner & Metzger (1983). On this subject, see, for example, also Aiello (1996), Lescarbeau, Payette, & St-Arnaud (1990), Lippitt & Lippitt (1986), and the more recent studies by De Haan (2006), Rossettie (2004), and Stroh & Johnson (2005).

[2] In service industries whose output is mainly made up of *intangibles* (data, information and knowledge), production and delivery can be said to be simultaneous and the various stages in the (production-) delivery process can be interpreted as the different stages involved in completing that output.

[3] For example, as will be seen in greater detail in Chapter Five, in the "almost-consulting model" diagnosing the problem is not part of the process in that the client has already done this before the consultant is called in. Whereas in the "classical model" the diagnostic and the therapeutic phases, are the central part of the process.

[4] In regard to which of the consultant's abilities the client deems to be most critical for the success of the consulting intervention, see, for example, Bobrow (1998b), Bowers & Degler (1999), Dowling (1993), Ford (1985), Hegyi-Gioia (1999), Kumar & Simon (2001), Popovich (1995), and Riley (1999). For a description of the main factors affecting the consulting process outcome, see Jang & Lee (1988), McLachlin (1999), and Schaffer (1997a; 1997b).

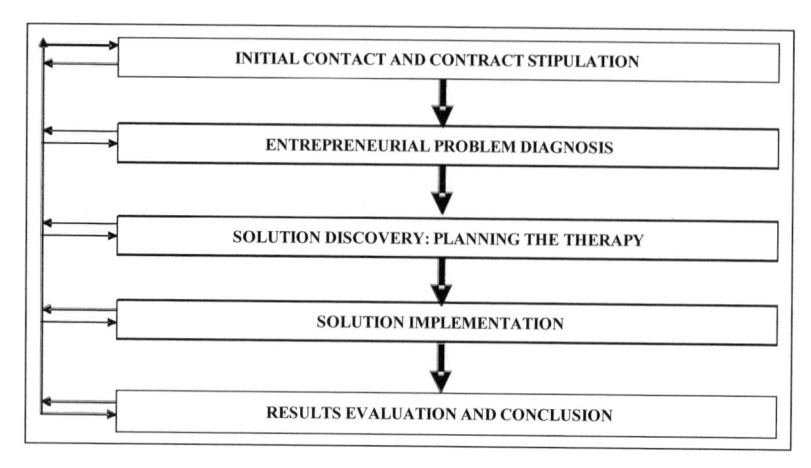

```
┌─────────────────────────────────────────────┐
│  INITIAL CONTACT AND CONTRACT STIPULATION   │
└─────────────────────────────────────────────┘
                      ↓
┌─────────────────────────────────────────────┐
│      ENTREPRENEURIAL PROBLEM DIAGNOSIS      │
└─────────────────────────────────────────────┘
                      ↓
┌─────────────────────────────────────────────┐
│   SOLUTION DISCOVERY: PLANNING THE THERAPY  │
└─────────────────────────────────────────────┘
                      ↓
┌─────────────────────────────────────────────┐
│            SOLUTION IMPLEMENTATION          │
└─────────────────────────────────────────────┘
                      ↓
┌─────────────────────────────────────────────┐
│       RESULTS EVALUATION AND CONCLUSION     │
└─────────────────────────────────────────────┘
```

Figure 5. The *diachronic* interpretation of management consulting: the consulting process.

1. Setting Up the Consulting Relationship

The setup phase sees the first contacts between consultant and client, and this triggers the mutual learning dynamics that will continue until the conclusion of the consulting process.

This stage is very delicate for both players. The clients need to manage the "main problem" for which the consulting service was required and, at the same time, they need to stay on top of the immediate problem, that of "purchasing the service" (choosing which consultant to engage). The task is physiologically complex for it is arduous to obtain adequate information. The consulting service is a "credence product", about which direct information is not immediately and directly available[5], and its attributes are not clearly discernible either before it is bought or, very often, in the first stages of the consulting process[6]. To make up for the scarcity

---

[5] The only information the client can obtain is indirect and mediated (e.g., the consultant's reputation or comparable consulting experiences related by other firms).

[6] On the purchase behavior of managing consulting services, see, for example, Edvardsson (1990).

of information, consultants have the difficult task of "gaining the client's trust"[7] (especially if this is a "new client") with particular reference to their professionalism, integrity and skills; and they must also ensure that they do not raise over-ambitious expectations about the possible outcomes of their intervention. Therefore, the initial contacts[8] should be directly handled by partners and/or senior managers from the consulting firm and their approach should not be excessively geared either to selling the service ("marketing-dominated" attitude) or to defining the detailed legal aspects of the assignment ("contractual" attitude).

How far the players involved are able to build a relationship based on trust and empathy[9], and to what extent they are aware

---

[7] See, for example, Czerniawska (2006a; 2007), Galford, Green, & Maister (2000a; 2000b), Green (2006), Kubr (2002), LaGrossa & Saxe (1998).

[8] The person requesting the consulting intervention is not necessarily the real "user" of the service. Even during the setup phase the consultant must then be able to obtain a clear picture of which people in the client firm will, directly or indirectly, play a part in the consulting process, and what part they will play. The following taxonomy may be useful:
1. *initial* clients. They make the first contact and take part in the setup phase;
2. *intermediate* clients. They join the consultant to take part in the various stages of the consulting process. They may be:
   – *reference* clients, i.e. the consultant's reference points in the client firm (the members of the client firm's staff in charge of the consulting process);
   – *end-user* clients, i.e. those who are most directly interested in the entrepreneurial problem being solved;
   – *actuation* clients, i.e. those who are actively involved in "putting into practice" (implementing) the consulting project;
   – *operational* clients, i.e. all the other persons in some way involved in the consulting process (e.g., knowledge providers, information support providers).
3. *primary* clients. They are the members of the client firm's top management (regardless of the extent to which they are directly involved in the consultant's work).

See also Ielo (1996) and Schein (1987) in this connection.

[9] As McLachlin (1999, p. 399) says "There must be a decent match of personality or management style (Shenson, 1990a), personal chemistry (Mitchell,

of the delicate psychological factors involved in the early contacts[10], is paramount if the consulting relationship is to "get off on the right foot". Important points to understand are that clients may show *symptoms of anxiety* because:

- they have high expectations of the consultant's ability to solve their problems, especially if these problems and the symptoms do not affect only one area, and if they have already triggered processes of deterioration of the physiological state of the firm ("the last beach" syndrome);
- they are also diffident as (especially in the early stages) they see the consultant as an "outsider", unconnected to the firm ("he is not one of us" syndrome).

Similarly, consultants have to deal with their own emotional tensions, generated by wondering if:

- there is an effective solution to the problem the client is describing;
- they can solve it. Every firm, and every business problem, is unique; and previous successes in comparable contexts do not guarantee that the consultant will be successful in the new assignment.

The parties' ability to establish a relationship based on mutual trust is vital since, even in the setup phase, the consultant conducts a *preliminary diagnosis*. The aim is not to analyze the consulting problem in depth, and is certainly not to

---

1994), and belief systems (Margolis, 1985)". That is the client and the consultant must try to work side by side in psychological harmony, and to establish some basis of shared meanings. In many cases, this is no easy task.

[10] "...the notion that rational models can satisfactorily explain interpersonal interaction seemed unrealistic, since they tend to ignore the 'human' factor. Personal styles of behavior, whether we like it or not, are rooted in personality traits, and play a key role in the consultant/client interactive processes" (Adamson, 2000, p. 24).

come up with an immediate solution. The preliminary diagnosis is the necessary preparation for all the later stages, and its purpose is to "discover" and understand the "surface of the problem"[11], through a critical analysis of a first set of data and information. Without an adequate (though synthetic) initial understanding of the problem it would be impossible to establish the realistic opportunities for a consulting intervention (Kubr, 2002). Especially when the consulting problem is complex, it is essential to make a critical assessment of the client's initial interpretation. This assessment very often leads to a redefinition and, by re-interpreting the evident and latent symptoms, the true nature and confines of the problem will be "re-discovered" (an ill-defined, or wrongly defined, problem is probably unsolvable[12]).

After the preliminary diagnosis, the consultant draws up the *intervention proposal* and the relevant *financial proposal*. The intervention proposal defines the object of the consulting intervention (the problem), sets out the objectives to be achieved, describes the intervention plan (tasks, phases, timing), and gives details about the roles, experience, abilities and qualifications of the consulting team that will carry out the project, and the roles assigned to the client firm's staff[13].

The client's decision to purchase the service[14] will not de-

---

[11] To understand the "surface of the problem", consultants need to make use of their previous experiences and of their intuitive skills to get a full picture of the problem with regard to the client firm's business and structure, and in relation to staff abilities and responsibilities, and to the firm's present economic and financial situation, and to its prospects and targets.

[12] See Note 17 in this connection.

[13] Experienced consultants know that inadequate planning regarding roles (tasks, responsibilities) to be undertaken by the client will lead to problems and misunderstandings in the later stages of the process. For example, there would be serious difficulties if the consultant assumed that the client would undertake a given course of action but failed to inform the client, who had not expected, or intended, to do anything of the kind.

[14] The literature has a wide range of studies on the criteria that the client firm's management should adopt for an effective evaluation of the

pend solely on the credibility of the proposed intervention plan. Other factors that influence its acceptance are:

- the reliability (in terms of skills/qualifications and, especially, of previous experience in comparable assignments) of the people who will actually carry out the consulting intervention;
- the criteria for the "price". It could be "a lump sum", or based on the time spent (and paid by the hour) by the consultant ("time taken"), or it could depend on the results obtained ("success fees"). This third option means that the consultant has to take a loss if the project is not successful; but it does help to build a relationship of mutual trust with the client, who sees that they have the same interests ("they are in it together")[15].

The setup phase is concluded when the *consulting contract is drawn up and signed*. The *formal* contract should be clear and comprehensive as this avoids any misunderstandings about the parties' commitments. However, both parties should be aware of the importance of a different type of agreement: a *psychological* pact that cannot be codified in a legal document but that confirms their sincere commitment to work together in a spirit of trust and respect, which is essential for the success of the entire consulting process.

---

consulting intervention proposals (e.g., Brotheridge & Power, 2007; Green, 1963), and, more in general, for the effective management of the whole consulting process (e.g., Fischer & Rabaut, 1992; Wells, 1983).

[15] Criteria for "success fees", and similar payments, are not easy to establish, because it is difficult to determine *ex post* which changes in the client firm's structure and business performance results are a direct consequence of the consulting intervention. Another difficulty is that (most of) the effects will be produced after the end of the consulting intervention. In this regard, see Section 5 in this Chapter.

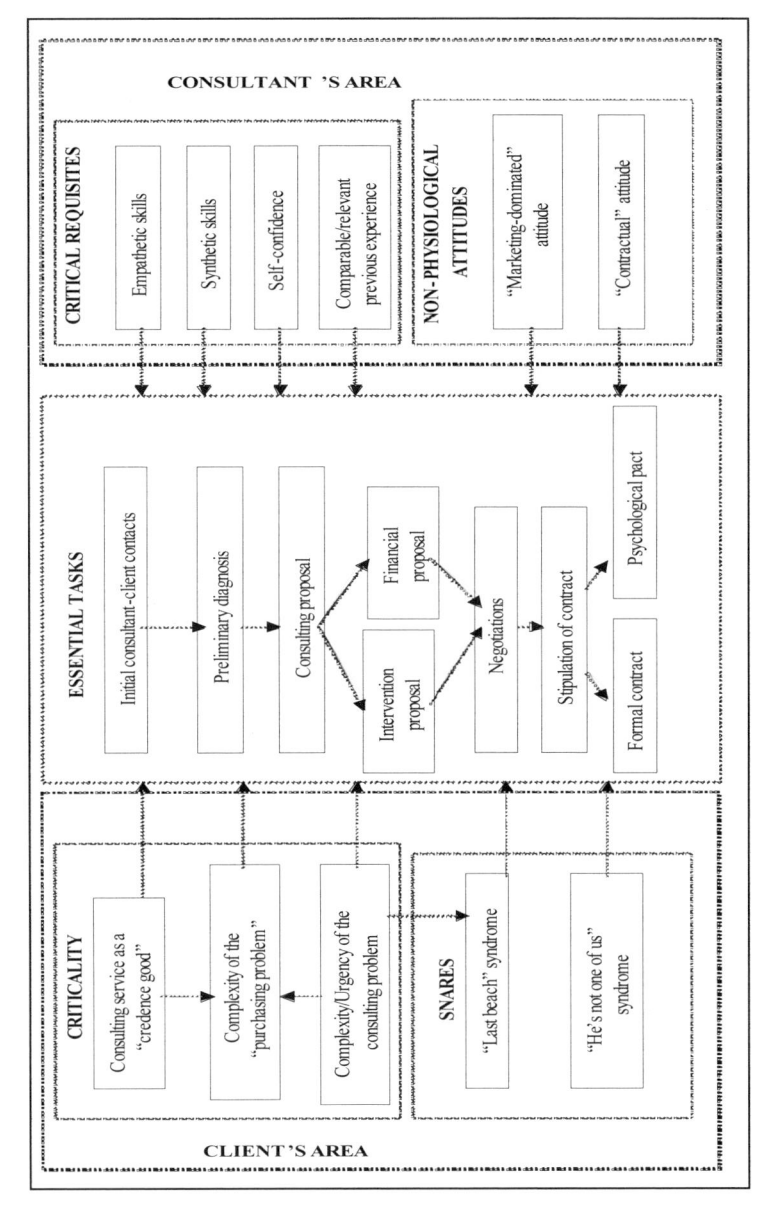

Figure 6. The setup phase of the consulting process: essential tasks, criticality and logical relations.

2. Diagnosing the Entrepreneurial Problem

This is the first stage in the consulting process to be prevalently "operational". After indications from the preliminary diagnosis, steps are taken to define the problem, to discover its causes, and to identify what resources/abilities the client has that could be useful in the solution process[16].

If we define *the substance of the problem* as being *the "gap" between the present (initial) state of the firm's structure*, or a realistically foreseeable state, *and the ideal (sought-for) state of this structure*, we can distinguish three problem categories:

- *correctional problems*. There is a *deteriorated present state* requiring interventions for a return to the *normal state*;
- *evolutionary problems*. The firm's structure needs to improve and develop, and the *sought-for state* is an *evolutionary improvement* of a mainly *normal initial state*;
- *creative problems*. It is necessary to deliver a *new and different state* (not simply a modification of the present one) that will replace the initial state (whether it was normal or deteriorated).

The consultant will usually be faced with a combination of the above types of problems. Frequently, the diagnostic analysis will also change the nature of the problem itself, for example by showing that a radical innovation of the deteriorated initial state should prove to be far better than its simple correction.

For the definition of the initial state of the firm's structure, *analytical skills* are the best asset to have, while the identification of the state to be aimed for, especially in the third problem category, requires *insight* and *creative skills*.

---

[16] On a conceptual level, diagnosing the problem does not include searching for a solution. However, practical consulting experience shows that cause analysis and the search for possible solutions are so very interdependent that they are never really effective unless tackled together. In this regard, see also Kubr (2002).

The diagnosis should also enable the consultant to *define the problem*[17] in terms of *organizational collocation* (hierarchical levels, functional areas and/or organizational units where the problem and the causes are located); *ownership* (hierarchical levels, functional areas and/or organizational units most affected by the solution of the problem); *intensity* (absolute and relative impact on the resource systems, on capabilities, on operational processes, and on overall synthesis results (Vallini, 1991)), and *time collocation* (duration, frequency of symptoms, past evolution and expected evolution).

To *identify the causes*, the consultant must deconstruct the problem, starting with an analysis of the symptoms manifested. The aim is to identify the significant cause-effect relationships between basic components. This work calls for the simultaneous application of analytical, synthetic, empathetic, and intuitive skills.

Analytical skills are indispensable for the deconstruction of the problem and the reconstruction of the system of cause-effect relationships between the significant variables[18]. The complexity of the entrepreneurial problem is affected by:

---

[17] A correct definition of the entrepreneurial problem can mean that the consultant will not solve "the wrong problem instead of the right problem, or alternatively ... the least important problems given the limited resources of the organization" (Kilmann, 1979, p. 32).

[18] Collecting and elaborating all the significant data and information is essential if the diagnosis is to be effective. There must be adequate selection criteria; and the data must be sufficiently detailed.
There are three main categories of information sources which can be used by consultants:
- company records which are already available or can specially be requested by the consultant (e.g., accounting records, and statistical records), giving data and information which can be read and transcribed, and are obtainable from the relevant storage support systems (hard copy or computer files, graphs, diagrams, etc.);
- direct observation of the company "at work", not only in terms of work conditions and methods, and production rates, but also attitudes, behaviors and interpersonal relation dynamics;
- data and information from company staff members regarding experiences, opinions, beliefs, prejudices, feelings, impressions, etc., obtainable through interviews and/or the administration of questionnaires.

- the quantity and intensity of the mutually influential relationships between the variables. Often, variables belonging to the substance of the problem influence one another and become at one and the same time both cause and effect (circular relationships);
- the length of the cause-effect chain. The final cause of the problem is always, in some way, related to the attitudes and abilities of the top management (if their decisions had been faultless, the problem would not have come into existence) and/or of the client firm's owners (as they appoint the senior managers and are responsible for seeing that they are effective);
- the articulation of the cause-effect chain (which measures the multiplicity of causes generating each effect and the multiplicity of effects stemming from each cause)[19].

Synthesis and intuitive skills are fundamental for the consultant to be able to identify the nature and direction of the relationships, and to identify the real causes and effects of the problem, by distinguishing between which of the variables involved are *relatively primary* and which are *relatively secondary*[20]. These

---

Since the final aim of the consulting intervention is to introduce changes, and as these changes are primarily cognitive in nature, direct observations and the anecdotal information from the questionnaires/interviews are absolutely essential as sources, and often have a greater impact on the final outcome of the intervention than the codified data sources.

[19] For an interesting example of a firm diagnostic check-up tool which incorporates some practices used by the main strategic consulting firms (for example, Bain and Company, Booz Allen & Hamilton, Boston Consulting Group), see Hagerty (1997).

[20] A number of different analytical methods can be adopted to identify relationships, proportions and (present and emerging) trends, and for other functions which the nature and purpose of the consulting assignment necessarily entail. These methods may be mathematical (equations that specify the relationships between variables, indexes that express input/output ratios or the internal structure of a particular variable, etc.);

skills are critical and very rare at one and the same time; and some people think that such skills can be developed, through the consulting experience, only in individuals endowed with innate intuitive talents[21].

It is essential the consultant be able to stimulate a collaborative environment (*empathetic skills*), which:

- encourages the client to be actively involved in the diagnostic process[22];
- can limit and then overcome any "evasive" or "antagonistic" attitudes in the client firm. Such attitudes (there may even be outright rejection of the consulting intervention)

---

they may be statistical (averages, dispersions, frequency distributions, correlations, regressions, etc.); or graphical (e.g., flow charts). Techniques for drawing comparisons (for comparing present and past, planned and delivered, firms in the same industry, etc.) are often essential. They are needed to obtain a full picture of the firm and of the consulting project, and to clarify the significance of the data and of the main variables.

If experimental research tools and methods could be used, this would undoubtedly make it easier to ascertain the existence, intensity and direction of the cause-effect relations between the significant variables. If we were able to remove one of the hypothetical causes and then test to see whether or not a given effect were still present, it would be possible to exclude (or confirm) that the primary cause had been isolated, for example. Unfortunately for the consultant, a firm is not a laboratory, and such experiments can rarely, if ever, be carried out.

[21] Sometimes, the synthesis of the problem can be arrived at deductively. For instance, the consultant "recognizes" similar patterns (forms) that had been seen in previous consulting projects (gestalt approach). However, this happens infrequently. Usually, most or part of the problem will be unique, or at least new for the consultant. In that case, only inductive methods can be adopted to discover what the problem is and where the primary causes lie; and this requires the skillful application of creative synthesis processes, and a great deal of insight.

[22] To this end, the consultant must be able to work closely with the client firm's staff from the very first phases of the consulting process. But more is needed: the firm's staff must be adequately informed and trained as to why a consulting intervention is necessary, how it will be carried out, and to achieve what aims.

are more frequent if the consulting model adopted is very dissimilar to the meta-consulting model[23];
- reduces the risk that the client may resort to spontaneous and/or premature attempts to correct the entrepreneurial problem being solved.

Being aware of what errors clients tend to make when assessing problems will help the consultant to recognize such errors, to escape being unduly influenced by them, and to avoid committing similar ones. Perhaps the most frequent error is *confusing the symptom with the problem.* But many errors are due to *preconceived ideas* (the client "knows" what the causes "must" be without having carried out the necessary investigations). Others stem from *over-specialized visions* (a mono-functional view of problems prevents one grasping the physiologically multi-disciplinary nature of corporate problems), or from *insufficient available time.*

An analysis of the client's problem-solving potential usually centers on:

- the client's degree of awareness of the problem;
- the client's real desire to solve the problem;
- the client's synchronic problem-solving potential: present resources, capacities, and skills that can be useful in solving the problem;
- the client's diachronic problem-solving potential: resources, capacities, and skills used to solve comparable problems in the past, and the potential for developing new resources, capacities, and skills that could be useful in the present problem.

The *diagnostic report* (listing the diagnostic steps taken and giving an analytical description of the problem, and of its direct and indirect causes) concludes this delicate phase of the consult-

---

[23] See Chapter Five in this connection.

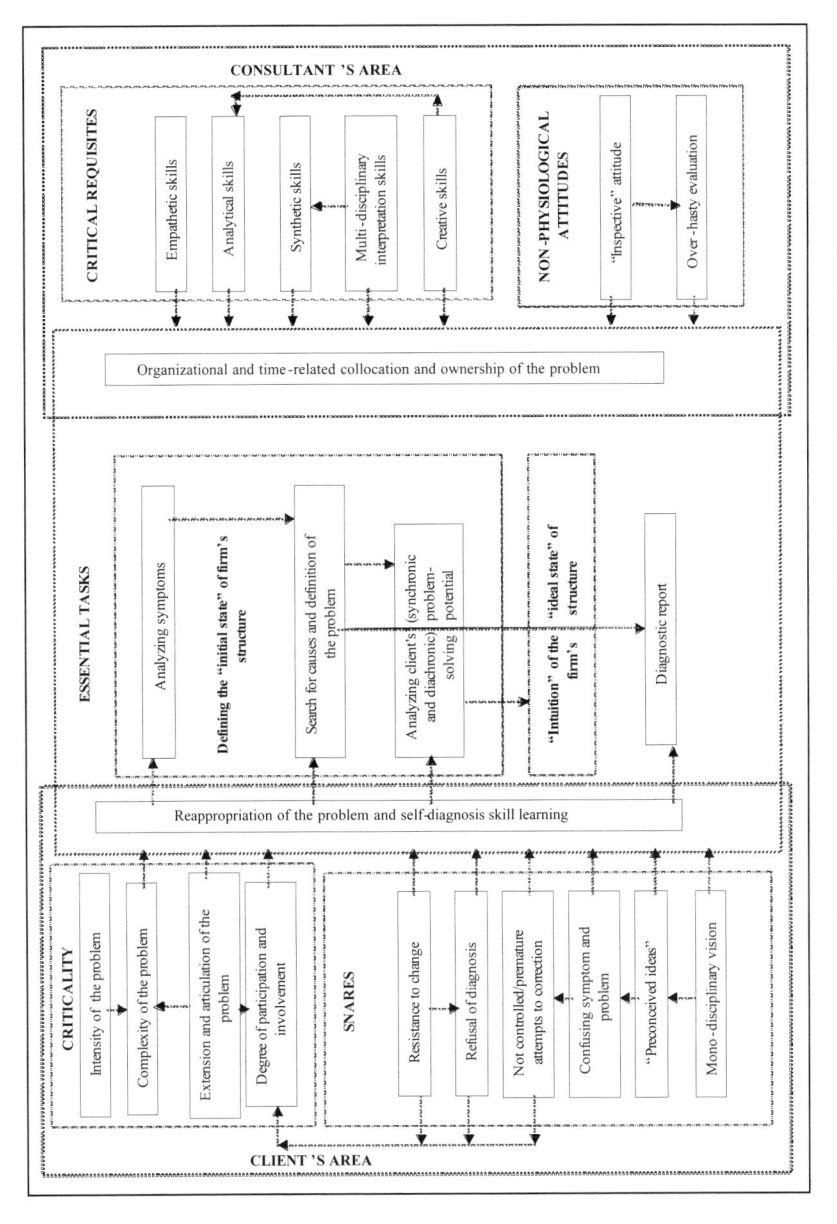

Figure 7. The consulting diagnosis: essential tasks, criticality and logical relations.

ing process, and makes it possible for the client and the consultant to check the logical and interpretive power of the analyses made (see Figure 7).

3. Planning the Therapy

Provided that the relationship is not broken off at the end of the diagnostic stage[24], in this phase the consultant identifies possible solutions to the problem diagnosed, evaluates their feasibility, assists the client in the choice of a solution, and programs its practical realization (Kubr, 2002).

The consultant's *creative skills* come into play for it takes real insight and vision to project a wide range of innovative solutions. It is these abilities that make the consultant an "agent of change" (Docherty, Stjernberg, & Werr, 1997).

It is not the consultant's task to find the "best solution of all" but to set in motion a problem-solving process, and to facilitate the search by providing the client with all the information required for a well-reasoned choice of the "best possible solution in the given corporate context". As it concerns the "not delegable entrepreneurial functions" (Ciampi, 2004; Fazzi, 1982) of the client firm's top-level managers[25], the decision about which solution to take cannot be delegated to anyone else inside the firm, and it certainly cannot be left to outsiders. It is the *sole property* of the client firm's top management, just as the problem itself is.

The active participation of clients in this phase means that:

- they can exploit their creative skills and abilities (which often make significant contributions to the solution); and

---

[24] One reason for breaking off the consulting process at the end of the diagnostic phase could, for example, be that clients think they are able to work out the solution without further outside help.

[25] See Chapter Three.

- a favorable organizational spirit of change can be created. This is essential if the consultant is to help the client to acquire new, autonomous *diagnostic* and *problem-solving skills* (Schein, 1987), and also to optimize the effects of the next stage (i.e. the implementation stage).

The consultants' *ability to identify possible solutions to the diagnosed problem* finds valid support in the *ability to interpret the organizational and strategic realities of firms*; an ability that can be mainly acquired through consulting experience. There are limits, however, to the recourse to solutions that have already been adopted in previous consulting interventions. The limits are connected to:

- the special nature of consulting service clientele, in the sense that every firm "has its own story", and its own particular characteristics, making it different from any other. The problems firms have to face are therefore unique, and, what is more, they want to find their own unique solutions;
- the nature of the problem to be solved. Of the three categories I set out, creative problems need more innovative solutions than evolutionary and correctional ones.

Hence, the consultant must know how to activate and manage cognitive processes for the co-operative generation of new ideas (and/or new combinations of ideas) through *creative thinking*[26] and *lateral thinking*[27]. These techniques induce the conscious, deliberate separation of the idea generating phase, from the phases of selection and analytical evaluation; and they encourage a situation of "suspended judgment" (giving free rein to

---

[26] In regard to creative thinking techniques (brainstorming, synergism, morphological analysis, etc.), see Rawilson (1981).

[27] In regard to lateral thinking techniques, see, for example, De Bono (1977; 1991).

one's thoughts is encouraged; all premature criticism of the generated ideas is excluded), and of unconditioned freedom ("lateral thinking" and "divergent thinking"). The goal is to bring to the surface as many ideas as possible (quantity not quality is the objective), even if these ideas seem unrelated to the problem itself, its causes, effects or the involved functional areas (generating "crazy ideas" is encouraged)[28].

The client and the consultant need to use their creative skills to the full; but to do this, they must be aware of the psychological barriers that may hinder their creative powers and make their cognitive processes for new idea generation less effective. There are several obstacles to creative thinking. If one is aware of them, they can be avoided and/or overcome. Some relate to:

- institutional (academic or otherwise) educational practices, which, especially in the West, tend to overemphasize analytical-rational thought, thereby discouraging the habit of using creative skills;
- the natural tendency to conform to our interlocutor's expectations (especially if he/she is deemed to be influential), so as to escape criticism or a possible refusal;
- insufficient available time. This causes anxiety and is hardly conducive to lateral thinking;
- individualism. This makes group work less effective (and sometimes impossible), thereby limiting the fertile exchange of ideas (*cross-fertilization*) that group work can spark off.

---

[28] In these cognitive processes a number of factors play a critical role, such as the feeling of frustration due to the apparently fruitless and inapplicable ideas that are aired; and also the attempts at idea "cross-fertilization" (combining dissimilar ideas) or the activation of incubation periods, whereby intentional creativity processes are broken off suddenly, and attention is focused on other activities, thus enabling people to "deposit" the problem in their subconsciouses. This weakens inhibitions and helps to remove emotional "blocks" toward new ideas, and lets people maximize their innate, untapped intuitive abilities, which may lead to unexpected insights and new, unthought of, solutions.

"Suspending judgment" is instrumental in generating innovative solutions. At some point, however, the problem-solving ideas identified need to be classified, *evaluated*, and *selected*[29]. Whatever the evaluation technique adopted (linear programming, decision analysis[30], etc.), it is useful to:

- avoid the temptation to invest excessive amounts of time and energy looking for the objectively ideal solution (which rarely exists), and instead to concentrate on comparing the solutions that seem satisfying and feasible;
- adopt models that:
  - can weight not only quantitative criteria (e.g., the cost of new machinery to modernize production systems) but also qualitative criteria (e.g., improvements in decision effectiveness through a change in the management's organizational structure model), by associating numerical values with adjectival scales; and
  - attribute weights so as to be able to compare heterogeneous evaluation criteria (e.g., economic criteria and organizational criteria).

Once the most feasible solutions have been evaluated and selected, the consultant draws up the *therapeutic plan* and presents it to the client. For each proposed solution, the plan should show:

- characteristics, advantages, drawbacks, risks, conditions to be created and maintained for the effectiveness of the solution; and
- a realistic implementation program (stages, procedures and decisions needed to make the solution operational; roles, tasks and responsibilities of client and consultant)[31].

---

[29] To evaluate the problem-solving potential of the ideas generated during the creative phase, there must be a return to rational thought processes (analytical thinking and "convergent thinking").

[30] On decision analysis models, see, for example, Ulvila & Brown (1982).

[31] A good therapeutic plan must establish not only *what* should be done but also *how* the plan should be realized.

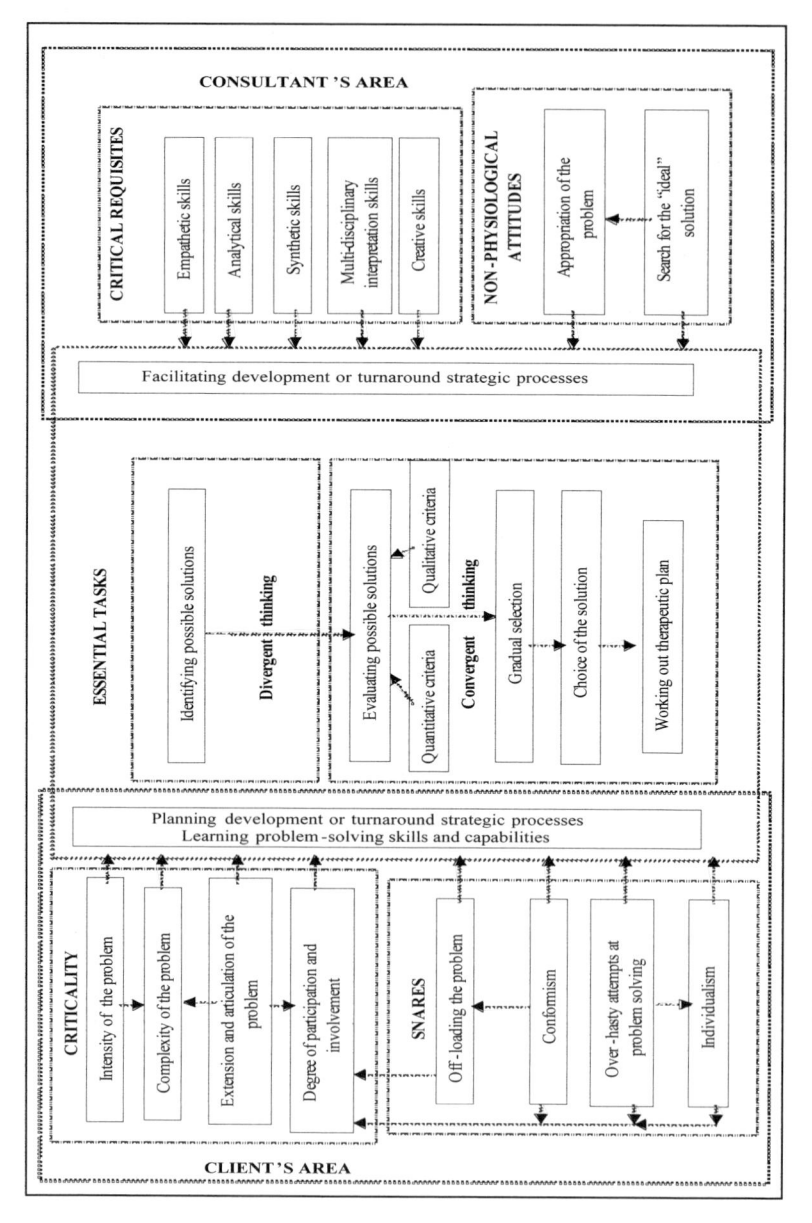

Figure 8. Planning the therapy: essential tasks, criticality and logical relations.

4. Implementing the Solution

Through the solution implementation stage, the proposed changes in the firm's structure are applied, and the programmed results are "put to the test".

Unless the therapeutic intervention is relatively simple, an adequate involvement of consultants in the realization stage[32] is fundamental[33]. That way they are spurred not to abandon the problem (and the client) before putting into practice worked out solutions[34] and making sure they work effectively. And they will also be less likely (in the early stages of the consulting process)

---

[32] In "real" consulting contexts, to what extent the consultant is involved in the implementation stage will depend primarily on the consulting model adopted (see Chapter Five), on the abilities and the time available to the consultant and the client, and on the type of problem to be solved.

[33] How effective the implementation stage is depends to a great extent on how well the consultant and the client cooperate in the earlier stages. If the client is not convinced by the plan, and/or if the consultant has worked out the plan on the basis of inexact and/or incomplete information, the chances of success are very slim.

[34] Often the ideal solution is to form mixed teams (i.e. made up of consultants and members of the client firm's staff) which include the people who were engaged in working out the therapeutic plan. This facilitates collaboration, participation, and commitment, by both the parties, regarding the new methods and techniques introduced through the consulting intervention. This solution also maximizes results in terms of the new knowledge and capabilities acquired by the client firm. If the meta-consulting model (see Chapter Five) is adopted, the client is now able to complete the learning process begun in the earlier stages of the process. There are two possible alternatives to a client-consultant joint solution implementation:
1. the client implements the solution independently; the consultant acts only as an outside supervisor. This option has financial advantages for the client. The inherent risk, however, is that the consultant may therefore be more likely, in the earlier stages, to "propose brilliant ideas that do not stand up, rather than truly functional solutions";
2. the whole solution implementation process is managed only by the consultant. Here, the main risk is that the client's executive and non-executive staff may be less willing to collaborate, or may even try to resist the implementation of the changes.

to propose "brilliant ideas that do not stand up rather than less brilliant but nonetheless thoroughly functional solutions"[35].

In this stage, the consultant must deal with the client's "cognitive gaps". In the sense that even when clients have taken an active part in the diagnostic and therapy-planning stages (and are sincerely convinced of the need for the agreed changes), they often tend to overrate the difficulties that come to light during the implementation phase, with the result that they soon lose faith in the new solution, no longer believe in the advantages it will bring, and think instead about returning to solutions that had been adopted in the past.

The management of these cognitive divergences may be facilitated:

- by a realistic, adequately organized and clearly defined therapeutic plan, and realistic schedules for its implementation. This will limit any setbacks when the plan is being put into practice; and it will also increase the client's awareness of the main obstacles to be overcome, and of the methods through which these obstacles can be faced;
- by programming guidance sessions aimed to specifically help the client to master methods, techniques and tools needed in the implementation of the solution;
- by careful monitoring the progress made in the intervention so as to avert setbacks, to limit the impact of ineluctable setbacks, and so that the client will not be (or feel) alone when an emergency arises, or when an unexpected situation is perceived as such;
- if the consultant behaves sensibly[36], so that he/she is perceived as a reassuring figure, a colleague with more

---

[35] The last decade has seen an increasing demand by large and medium-sized firms for consulting interventions to focus mainly on solution implementation (e.g., Poulfelt, Greiner, & Bhambri, 2005).

[36] While the diagnostic and therapeutic planning phases require analytical abilities, intelligence and creativity, the implementation stage requires, above all, "courage" and "self-confidence".

experience, who is enthusiastic and fully committed, who shares the responsibilities and has a clear vision of what the intervention aims should be and the ability to explain this to the others involved in the project (Kubr, 2002).

Some solutions that may maintain an active involvement of the consultant, yet at the same time keep the overall costs of the consulting intervention down, are:

- a gradual reduction in the consultant's involvement based on the progress made in the realization phase;
- active participation by the consultant only in the critical stages of the implementation process;
- scheduling regular meetings (between consultant and client) so that the consultant can monitor the progress of the intervention and suggest possible adjustments and corrections.

Experienced consultants agree that the effectiveness of the solution implementation process depends to a great extent on how well the timing of the changes is managed. The following points are crucial:

- beginning the implementation stage before the solution scheme is clearly defined and agreed upon may have advantages for the therapy planning process (the adoption of a number of different solution schemes enables one to test more than one solution and to learn through "trial and error"). But the end-result will be a greater divergence between the definitive therapy programmed and the clients' behavior in that they will be inclined to resort to one or more of the methods which were tried out and discarded (especially those they had themselves suggested);
- "pacing the change": how quickly the changes are put into practice, and how well this is managed, will affect

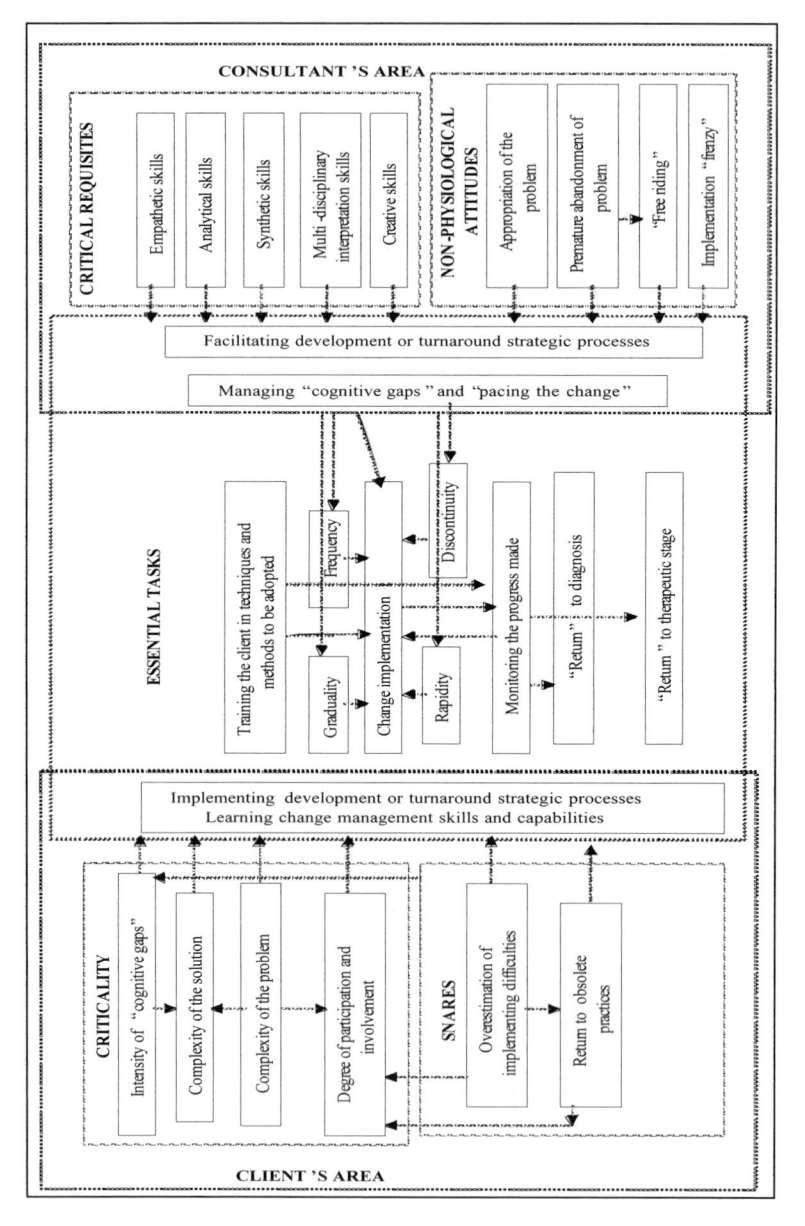

Figure 9. Implementing the therapy: essential tasks, criticality, and logical relations.

the solution's effectiveness. Quicker, more lasting, and generally better results are achieved by introducing the change gradually, in successive, relatively short stages, which are alternated with adequate consolidation periods (the interventions should be quick and frequent, but discontinuous and gradual)[37].

5. Evaluating Results and Concluding the Process

When and how the relationship is concluded is by no means irrelevant for an assessment of the overall success of the consulting intervention.

It is true that the relationship may be ended early because of a unilateral decision by the client, who is dissatisfied with the consultant's work. But more frequent reasons for termination before the objectives have been fully achieved are that:

- the client firm is able to carry out the remaining stages of the change process autonomously (early termination);
- one or both of the parties may overrate the client's ability to conclude the process independently (premature termination);
- the consultant leaves the project due to lack of time, or for causes unconnected to the relationship (the consultant "takes off") [38].

Late termination of the relationship (after the initially scheduled termination point) happens most frequently:

---

[37] I am in agreement with analysts like Schaffer (1997a; 1997b) who stress the importance of scheduling and achieving intermediate goals, with improvements that can easily be measured, are incremental and rapidly deliverable, rather than concentrating only on general, wide-ranging objectives.

[38] If the consultant "takes off", the client may feel frustrated (because the programmed assignment has not been completed) and/or may feel less able to run the firm and take decisions ("separation syndrome").

- because of deficiencies and/or dysfunctions in one or more of the process stages (e.g., deficiencies in the diagnostic stage), which generate the need for procedures that were not initially programmed (e.g., the need to diagnose new problems that come to light during the implementation stage). This increases the duration (and the cost) of the consulting intervention;
- because the consultant slows down the process through incomplete transfer of knowledge, or by "creating" inexistent problems and/or exaggerating real problems, for example. The behaviors may be opportunistic (the consultants try to make themselves indispensable and/or to make the assignment longer), or may be due to judgment/evaluation errors and/or incompetence.

Late termination may leave clients feeling frustrated, too, (because the objectives have not been achieved within the time limits scheduled); and it may also cause them to become overdependent, and unable to take decisions without the reassuring presence of the consultant ("separation syndrome")[39].

Monitoring and evaluating the consulting intervention serves to determine to what extent the therapeutic plan's objectives have been achieved, and to check that the results achieved are consistent with the resources used. Evaluation should take place during the solution implementation stage (progressive valuation) so that contingency measures can be taken quickly if necessary, but also when the intervention is concluded (end valuation), and also after the conclusion (follow-up valuation).

Evaluating management consulting interventions is complex[40] for many different reasons, some of which are:

---

[39] In addition to choosing the "right time to leave", the consultant should also consider that a "gradual withdrawal" may be advisable in that there would then be less risk of the client wanting to "go it alone" either too soon, or not soon enough.

[40] Both consultant and client need to take an active part in the evaluation process, with mutual trust and the willingness to give merit where it is due

- it is difficult to identify which effects on the firm's structure and performance derive directly from the consulting intervention. There may, for example, be interferences caused by entrepreneurial problems and/or decisions unconnected to the field of the consulting intervention, or by changes in the firm's environment (changes in market trends, in the competitive field, etc.);
- the consulting intervention will have a natural tendency to affect many features in the client firm's structure and behavior; and the full effects tend to be seen in the medium- and long term. This is especially true of complex interventions;
- it is difficult to evaluate the "qualitative" effects of the intervention (knowledge and capabilities acquired by the client firm, improvements achieved in the firm's competitive strategies, changes in the firm's image and standing, etc. (e.g., Kubr, 2002));
- it is difficult to evaluate the effects on the consulting firm's competences and capabilities (wider knowledge, better image, etc.).

The consulting process is concluded when the consultant presents the final report, which summarizes all the measures taken and the results obtained in the different stages of the process, with specific details regarding:

- the objectives effectively achieved. Not only those directly related to the solution of the problem for which the assignment was given (e.g., a return to a given level

---

and to recognize one's own mistakes and shortcomings. Diverse authors have discussed how difficult it is to objectively evaluate and measure the real effects of management consulting interventions, for example Engwall & Kipping (2002a), Ernst & Kieser (2002; 2003), and Wright & Kitay (2002).

Other authors (e.g., Faust, 2002; Sturdy, 2002) underline the fact that the client takes an active role in evaluating the knowledge generated/transferred through the management consultant's intervention.

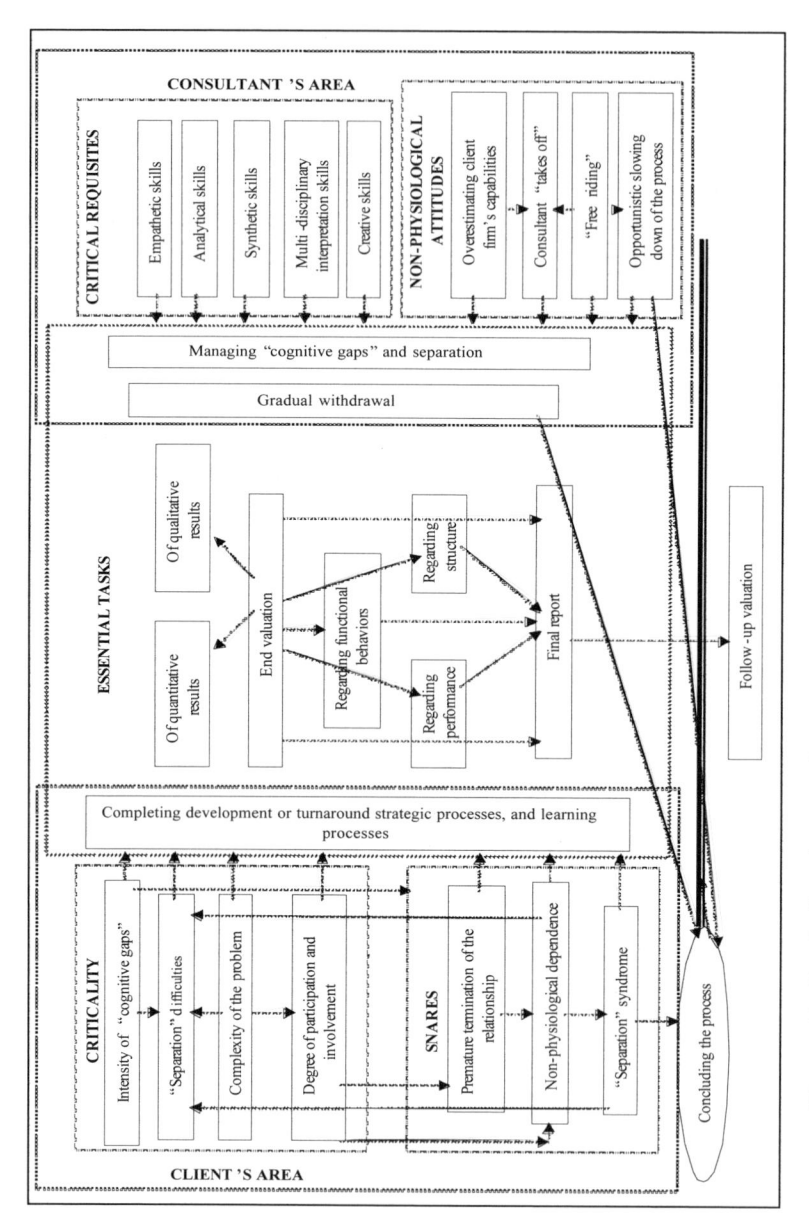

Figure 10. Concluding the consulting process: essential tasks, criticality and logical relations.

of productive efficiency), but also indirectly induced achievements (e.g., the development of new skills and capabilities in a given functional area); and
- the consultant's recommendations regarding criteria for the future utilization, monitoring and further development of the implemented solution. These recommendations aim to consolidate the new state of the client firm's structure which has been achieved through the consulting process.

Chapter Five

The Synchronic Interpretation: the Consulting Models

By focusing on the specific features of each phase, the *diachronic* approach (consulting process) does not reveal the overall picture of the essential variables of the relational dynamics on which the cognitive (i.e. knowledge creation) value, and hence the full success of the consulting relationship, depends. The consultancy process tends to take place with varying degrees of looping and reiteration, of completeness, and of intensity regarding client-consultant cooperation. The differences will depend on the required service configuration, on the entrepreneurial problem to be solved, on the ways the service is delivered and, above all, on the *consulting model* adopted (the *synchronic interpretation* of management consulting; see Ciampi, in press-b).

The *nature of the relationship* established and developed between the consultant and the client is key to the *synchronic interpretation* of management consulting. A number of factors become particularly relevant, such as the structure (i.e., the system of qualitative and quantitative features) of the entrepreneurial problem to be solved, the volume of specific investments required from both parties, the mainly codified or tacit nature[1] of

---

[1] *Codified knowledge* is knowledge that can be communicated and stored by way of appropriate codes or languages. As it can be "put down in black and white", this type of knowledge can be transmitted and used also by individuals (or organizations) other than those it was produced by. The fundamental sciences (chemistry, physics, etc.) and the engineering sciences (chemical engineering, aeronautical engineering, etc.) are typical examples of codified knowledge systems. Scientific articles and publications are manifestations of the codification and transmission, through codes and languages, of scientific discoveries. *Tacit knowledge* cannot be "put down in black and white", be-

the starting knowledge they own, the nature of the knowledge generated and transferred through the relationship, and the intensity of the knowledge generation/transfer dynamics.

The quality and quantity of the client's starting knowledge base are critical, as is the degree to which the consultant is inclined, and able, to activate and manage knowledge creation/transfer processes. Many different possible combinations have been identified in the literature regarding the forms that these features may assume (Maister, 1993; Schein, 1987; 1988; 1999). Here, I shall simply present three of the possible combinations, which, I

cause it has no codes or languages. This type of knowledge can be transferred from one organization to another only by "moving" the subjects that generated the knowledge. For example, knowledge pertaining to "experience" can be transferred from one firm to another only by physically moving the persons that have the knowledge. It is more difficult, consequently, to spread tacit knowledge, and the costs and constraints are much higher than with explicit knowledge. However, much of the competitive success of business organizations rests on the availability of this type of knowledge. For instance, a firm's competitive advantage can often be sustained only if new tacit knowledge is continually created and if this knowledge is turned into gradual technical (product or process) improvements. These knowledge creation dynamics depend on the experience and/or learning abilities of specific individuals and/or teams of individuals. To summarize, we can say that:
   a. codified knowledge is easier (and cheaper) to transfer than tacit knowledge. Consequently, it spreads much more rapidly outside the firm (than tacit knowledge does);
   b. because of the ease and speed with which it can be transferred and disseminated, codified knowledge is much more difficult to appropriate than tacit knowledge. By appropriation of knowledge, I mean the ability of the individual or organization (that has generated the knowledge) to prevent other individuals, or organizations, from using it for economic purposes;
   c. consequently, firms are not particularly stimulated to invest in the production of codified knowledge. They are stimulated to a much greater extent to invest in the production of tacit knowledge because its high level of appropriability guarantees there will be ample opportunities for "monopolistic profits" through which they will recover the capital invested.

See also Chapter Six and Arrow (1962).

believe, can be seen as theoretical configurations (models). Each is a conceptual abstraction that, as such, tends to take a different form in each specific consulting context[2]. Each model identifies a different "mode of reasoning" and a different "way to relate to the client" that the management consultant may adopt (see Figure 11).

Under the *almost-management consultancy* model, the client firm needs specific information and/or cognitive support to implement solutions to already diagnosed problems. The client company has already identified the problem, the type of intervention required for its solution, and the consultant to be engaged. After having established the need for a specific input of information or expertise in a given area, the client firm concludes that it does not have the capability to implement the solution on its own, or it concludes that it is more economically or politically[3] convenient to outsource it.

From the outset, the client-consultant interaction is highly structured with regard to mutual role expectations. This model assigns a critical role to the client firm, as it must have the capability to:

- diagnose the problem autonomously;
- identify the solution autonomously;
- identify the specific information and/or expertise needed;

---

[2] In the course of the consulting process, the consulting model adopted may undergo various types of metamorphoses, which may lead to a spontaneous (or programmed) change in the consultant's role. The change may be from a passive role (the consultant simply supplies data and information requested by the client) to an active role (consultant and client work "side by side" to solve the problem), to a maieutic role (the consultant helps the client firm to develop the necessary capabilities to "cure itself").

[3] Some authors believe that the consultant's main roles include being a:
- "certifier" of the reasonableness of decisions taken by the client firm's management (Ernst & Kieser, 2002; Ruef, 2002);
- an assistant to the managers who engaged the consulting firm, in the organization's internal power struggles (Penn, 1998).

	"ALMOST-CONSULTING" MODEL	"CLASSICAL" MODEL	"META-CONSULTING" MODEL
CLIENT'S NEEDS	THE CLIENT IDENTIFIES THE PROBLEM AND ITS POSSIBLE SOLUTION. IMPLEMENTING THE SOLUTION REQUIRES SPECIFIC INFORMATION AND/OR SPECIALIZED EXPERTISE	THE CLIENT PERCEIVES SYMPTOMS OF CERTAIN DYSFUNCTIONS BUT IS UNABLE EITHER TO DIAGNOSE THE PROBLEM OR TO IDENTIFY A THERAPY	THE CLIENT PERCEIVES SYMPTOMS OF CERTAIN DYSFUNCTIONS, DOES NOT HAVE SELF-DIAGNOSIS CAPABILITIES, BUT WISHES TO DEVELOP THEM
CONSULTANT'S ROLE	THE CONSULTANT PROVIDES SPECIALIZED EXPERTISE AND/OR IMPLEMENTS THE SOLUTION	THE CONSULTANT DIAGNOSES THE PROBLEM AND DISCOVERS THE THERAPY	THE CONSULTANT "HELPS THE CLIENT TO HELP HIMSELF" (THUS FACILITATING THE DEVELOPMENT OF THE CLIENT'S SELF-DIAGNOSIS ABILITIES)

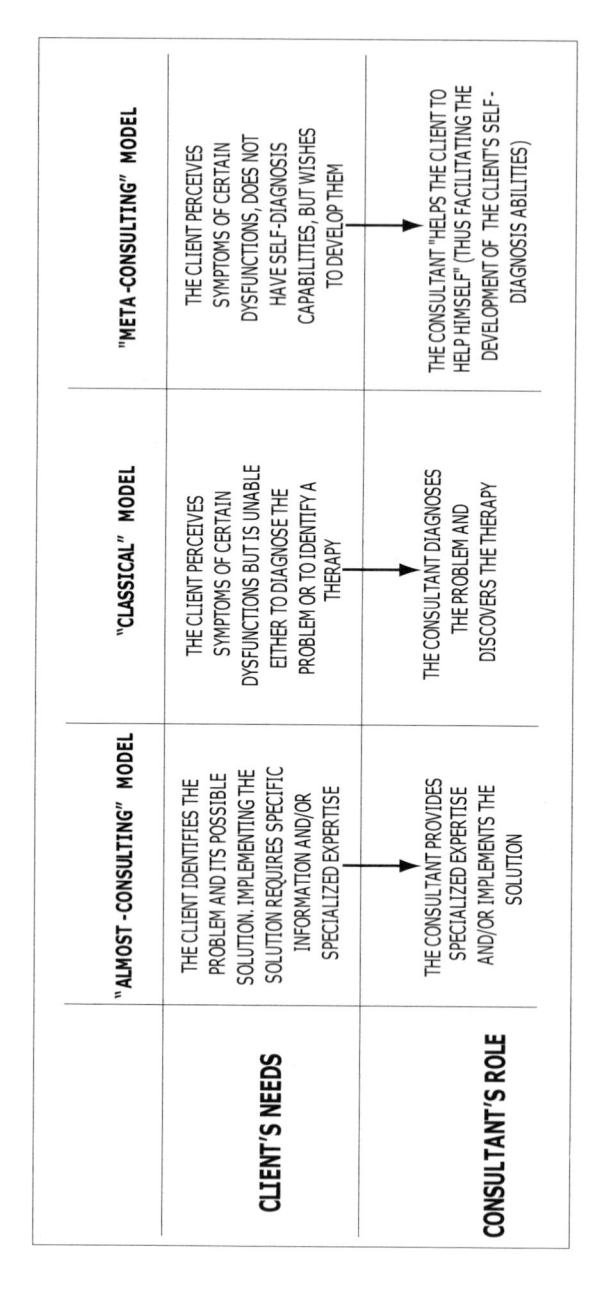

Figure 11. The *synchronic* interpretation of management consulting: consulting models.

- select the consultant that possesses the information and expertise needed[4];
- correctly communicate the problem to the consultant[5].

The consultant, whose role is merely that of a "knowledge provider", is required to possess *specialized expertise within the specific area* with which the consultancy intervention has to deal. The transferred knowledge mainly travels in the consultant⇨client direction, and takes on an almost exclusively codified character. The consultant's intervention has only a slight impact on the client firm's structure and therefore remains on the borderlines of management consulting work[6].

With the *classical* model, the company perceives symptoms of certain dysfunctions, but is unable to clearly spell out the scope of the problem, and is in no way able to identify the most appropriate solutions. The responsibility for conducting the diagnosis (problem finding) and subsequently identifying and suggesting the solution (problem solving) therefore falls to the consultant, who is given broad margins of freedom by the client. The client completely relies on the consultant and the remit is not only to find a remedy but also, and above all, to define the "borderlines of the disease". The diagnostic phase can sometimes carry the process to unexpected destinations, and may identify problems that are very different from the generic expectations that had originally led to the engagement. The relationship is much less

---

[4] If the evaluation of the knowledge required to solve the problem is the client firm's responsibility, and if the firm chooses a consultant who does not have this knowledge, then the firm will have to accept responsibility for the limited results that can be achieved (Schein, 1987).

[5] An unsatisfactory outcome to the consulting relationship is often due to the fact that the consultant did not fully understand the nature of the problem to be solved.

[6] One example of an almost-consulting relationship is when a firm lacks the necessary competencies to launch a new product in a particular geographical area, the project can be postponed no further, and the firm entrusts the consultant with the implementation of the launch.

structured, and its effectiveness is greatly influenced by the client's willingness (and capability) to become involved in the various phases of the consulting process [7]. While the client should be involved as intensely as possible, in principle, the more complex the problem, the more necessary is active client cooperation from the very first phases of the interaction (by a joint diagnosis of the dysfunctions, the problem is correctly reconfigured). The generated and transferred knowledge is mainly codified but, in contrast to what happens in the *almost-management consulting* model, the transfer is bidirectional (consultant⇔client). For the classical model to perform effectively:

- the client must provide the consultant with all the information needed to conduct a reliable diagnosis and must, above all, be ready to accept and manage the changes proposed by an in-depth diagnostic analysis "from the outside". Ontologically, this analysis is *per se* an intervention in that it brings about changes in the client firm's cognitive system[8]. If these changes are not adequately designed and managed, they may generate varying degrees of resistance and diffidence, especially in the functional areas most involved. The worst case scenario is that the ensuing defensive behaviors, and fall in motivation, will aggravate the problem, increase the symptoms and spread the causes and effects more widely;
- the consultant's *analytical, synthetic, and intuitive/creative skills* must be adequate for the complexity of the entrepreneurial problem to be solved. The consultant must also be *able to correctly communicate the diagnosis* to the

---

[7] The clients' capability depends mainly on their previous experiences (for example, the client may have already used the consultant's services). The clients' willingness is closely connected to their entrepreneurial culture and psychological mindset (for example, if they want to use the consultant simply "to get rid of the problem", then the desire to collaborate will be minimal). See Aiello (1995) in this regard.

[8] See Section 2 in Chapter Four.

client[9]. The consultant's analytical skills are indispensable for breaking down the entrepreneurial problem into its component parts and reconstructing the system of cause-effect relations among the principal explanatory variables. The consultant's synthetic, intuitive and creative skills are decisive for the correct identification of the primary causes of the problem and for there to be real insight into possible solutions;
– the client must understand and properly interpret the diagnosis made by the consultant, and must effectively be able to adopt the proposed solution ("cure")[10]. In the set-up stage of the consulting process, neither the consultant nor the client is in a position to foresee the final results. And especially when the entrepreneurial problem is particularly complex, clients are sometimes bewildered by the diagnosis made (as this may go against much, or even most, of their expectations regarding the nature of the problem) and also by the therapy proposed which, even though theoretically correct, might not be viable because of conflict with the value system and/or with the deep strategic identity of the client firm. In that case, the client firm will be unable (or, more often, unwilling) to implement the solution proposed by the consultant.

In conclusion, the *classical* model is appropriate provided that the client firm ("patient") is willing to rely wholly on the consultant ("physician") with regard both to the diagnosis and

---

[9] Despite the importance of a transparent and correct communication of the conducted diagnosis, empirical evidence shows that some consultants, on the contrary, deliberately use "obscure" or "sophisticated" language, assuming, often wrongly, that they will so win over the unconditional trust of the client.

[10] Obviously, if the client lacks either the abilities and/or the real desire to implement the change proposed by the consultant, then the consulting intervention is doomed to failure (Ginsberg, 1986; Jang & Lee, 1998; Kolb & Frohman, 1970; Rynning, 1992; Turner, 1982).

the therapy, is willing to implement the prescribed measures ("to take the medicine"), and to give up the idea of developing autonomous self-diagnosis and problem solving capabilities[11].

The *meta-consultancy* model is the most ambitious one: the client retains full ownership of the problem in every phase of the consultancy process in the assumption that no one knows more about the firm's strategic, managerial and cultural context than the client, and, consequently, no one is better placed to determine the real scale of the problem and the true feasibility and effectiveness of any possible solution interventions. The starting point is similar to the one in the classical model[12]: the client perceives certain shortcomings and dysfunctions, but is not able to pinpoint their origin, does not know how to deal with them, and finds it difficult to choose the most appropriate consultant. However, the degree of client involvement is far higher in every phase of the consulting process, particularly from the cognitive point of view. The consultant plays a "leading role" in the diagnosis (which nevertheless remains within the client's responsibility), acts as a "facilitator" for the solution discovery and implementation phases, and may also suggest recourse to further (external and/or internal) specialist resources if these are deemed necessary. The problem remains the client firm's[13], and the work of the consultant consists of "helping the client to help himself",

---

[11] One example of a "classical model" consulting relationship is when a firm perceives symptoms of financial tension (e.g., a progressive drop in the cash flow) but knows that turnover and profit margins are going well. The consultant will identify the problem (perhaps accounts receivables have exceeded physiological levels) and the solution (e.g., reduce sales to customers that do not keep to agreed settlement dates).

[12] It may, and frequently does, happen that relationships start out following the classical model but evolve toward the meta-consulting model.

[13] The literature (e.g., Armenakis & Burdg, 1988; Eccles, Shapiro, & Soske, 1993; Greiner & Nees, 1985; Madigan & O'Shea, 1997; Mitchell, 1994; Payne, 1986; Shenson, 1990a) makes ample reference to the fact that the client firm is the sole "owner" of the problem and must retain control over the consulting process at every stage; and that it must take the final responsibility for the outcome of the process.

by appealing to the client firm's present aptitudes and capabilities and supporting it in creating new aptitudes and capabilities. From the initial phases the consulting process is designed to fuel and develop the client firm's self-diagnosis and problem-solving capabilities, by implementing bidirectional (consultant⇔client) transfers of mainly "process" (i.e., tacit) knowledge. In conclusion, the meta-consulting intervention does not only aim to maximize the possibilities of solving the immediate problem. It goes much further, and the main purpose is to enable the client firm's top management to enhance its own level of autonomy when dealing with future entrepreneurial problems (Schein, 1987). Necessary conditions for effective meta-consultancy are:

- from the outset, the client firm must be aware of its responsibilities connected with retaining full ownership of the problem;
- the consultant must resist the temptation to free the client of the problem (Schaffer, 1997a; 1997b) and, at least in the initial phases, must avoid offering personal diagnostic interpretations, in order not to hamper the development potential of the client firm's self-diagnosis capabilities;
- in addition to analytical, synthetic and creative skills the consultant must also be endowed with *maieutic* and *empathetic skills* that can stimulate a high level of involvement of the client even in the early stages, thereby triggering cooperative processes for self-diagnostic and solution discovering techniques learning. The consultant's capacity to stimulate a collaborative and participatory relational environment is essential to overcome any "evasive" and/or "antagonistic" attitudes (or even outright "rejection"), which are physiologically present, particularly in people who hold positions in organizational areas where the root cause of the problem lies[14]. Hence consultants need to

---

[14] Attitudes of antagonism and/or rejection toward a diagnosis "coming from the outside" are most frequently present in client firms whose culture has a strong in-built "resistance to change".

avoid aggressive diagnostic attitudes that might give the impression of "hunting for mistakes to punish" ("inspective attitude") or that lead to premature value judgments, which may prevent clients from offering their own autonomous evaluations. Jointly conducting a shared diagnostic experience facilitates the diagnostic process. Clients know the problem better, but being over-involved they may be unable to "see the wood for the trees"; the agreement between client and consultant on the outcomes of a joint diagnosis emerges in a wholly natural way, without the need for the consultant to convince the client about its soundness. In addition, jointly conducting a shared diagnostic experience has an "ontological intervention value" in itself because it triggers a change in the client firm's cognitive system, which, by reacting to the stimuli, sets in motion processes for gradual "slatentization" and "re-appropriation" (and hence "control recovery") of the problem. These cognitive processes also enable the client firm to learn some of the consultant's diagnostic techniques and hence acquire new capabilities reusable in the future to solve problems autonomously, even problems which are not necessarily similar to those directly addressed in the consulting intervention;

– the client firm must be strongly motivated to develop autonomous problem-solving capabilities and must effectively be able to implement the related learning processes. The client firm's cognitive flexibility (i.e., its receptiveness to change and its ability to challenge its culture and working methods) is essential to ensure the effectiveness of the knowledge generation process set in motion in the course of the meta-consultancy intervention[15].

---

[15] One example of a meta-consulting relationship is the following. A firm realizes there are some inconsistencies in its competitive position. The consultant helps the client to identify what is wrong, by the joint construction and experimentation of models, methods and techniques for competitive position analysis, for competitor analysis, for the analysis of competitive trends,

Over the past ten years we have commissioned more than twenty different consulting firms to carry out more than forty strategic consulting projects. In the last five years, despite the fact that we have almost doubled our turnover and that the managerial complexity of our business has certainly grown, we have only implemented two consulting projects within the strategic field (one on the "redefinition of our concept of customer loyalty" and the other on the "redefinition of our value chain") using only one consultancy firm, Beta S.p.a. The fact is that after the first consulting project carried through by Beta S.p.a. our managers began to consider it possible to develop their own autonomous capacities to define, diagnose and solve problems, even when those problems belonged to completely new strategic contexts from those experienced in the past. For us, the risk of failure became a challenging opportunity for developing these capacities, an occasion that all the managers in our group are anxious to address, and no longer something from which to defend themselves, avoiding the problem as far as possible or offloading it onto external "specialists". The consultancy projects implemented by Beta S.p.a. are much more demanding than those implemented previously and cost almost twice as much. But the value they enable us to create in terms of new strategic and managerial skills and capabilities is immeasurably higher.

This revealing comment was made by the chairman of a multinational corporation working in the clothing industry, which owns three world-famous high-fashion labels and were reported to me by two partners of Beta S.p.a., a medium-sized Italian strategic consultancy firm that adopts intervention techniques consistent with the model we have defined as *meta-consulting*.

Figure 12 offers a synoptic picture of the essential features qualifying each of the three consultancy models described above.

etc. However, the consultant lets the client pinpoint the inconsistencies and organize the repositioning process. That way, the consultant helps the client firm to improve its strategic decision-taking capabilities.

Essential features	ENTREPRENEURIAL PROBLEM				CLIENT FIRM				CONSULTANT		CONSULTING RELATIONSHIP				INDUCED/SOUGHT EFFECTS	
	Breadth/ complexity	Diagnosis	Therapy	Cure	Initial knowledge about the problem	Critical capabilities	Critical features and propensities	Primary role	Critical skills	Primary role	Degree of structuring	Nature of generated and transferred knowledge	Knowledge transfer flows	Degree of client involvement	Primary goal	Primary risk
ALMOST-CONSULTING	Limited	Client responsible	Client responsible	Consultant mainly responsible	High	Diagnostic capability; Problem-solving capability; Capability to specify needed information/knowledge; Capability to select consultant; Capability to communicate the problem	Propensity to "offload the problem"	Acquirer of codified information (delegating solution implementation)	Specialized expertise regarding the specific consulting problem	Supplier of codified knowledge (implements the solution)	High	Essentially codified (content related)	One-way (consultant to client)	Limited	Mainly operational (implementing the problem solution)	High level of client dependency on consultant
CLASSICAL	High	Consultant mainly responsible	Consultant mainly responsible	Client mainly responsible	Limited	Capability to understand the consultant's diagnosis; Capability to implement the therapy	Information transparency; Propensity to change; Willingness to comply with consultant's "prescription"	Implementer of the prescribed treatment ("patient")	Analytical skill; Synthetic skill; Creative skill; Ability to communicate the diagnosis	Diagnostic and therapeutic role (appropriates the problem)	Limited	Mainly codified (mainly content related)	Two-way (consultant⇔client)	High	Entrepreneurial-technical (solving the problem)	Inconsistency between "prescription" and strategic identity of the client
META-CONSULTING	Very high	Client mainly responsible	Client mainly responsible	Client mainly responsible	Very limited	Cooperative learning capability	Awareness of "full ownership" of the problem; Cognitive flexibility; Motivation to learn; Desire to change	Cooperative learning protagonist	Analytical skill; Synthetic skill; Creative skill; Empathetic skill; Maieutic skill	Cooperative learning facilitator (remains outside the problem)	Very limited	Mainly tacit (mainly process related)	Two-way (consultant⇔client)	Very high	Entrepreneurial-cognitive (developing the client firm's self-diagnosis and problem solving capabilities)	Inconsistency between cognitive potential and client's capacity/will to learn

Figure 12. Consulting models: essential features of intervention object (entrepreneurial problem), parties in the relationship (client and consultant), consulting relationship, and outcomes (induced/sought effects).

Chapter Six

The Cognitive Interpretation: Meta-Consulting Knowledge Creation Pathways

1. Nonaka and Takeuchi's Organizational Knowledge Conversion Spiral

1.1. The Dimensions of Knowledge

Nonaka and Takeuchi (1995) define a firm's knowledge creation capacity as the capacity of an organization as a whole to generate new knowledge, to disseminate it internally and translate it into products, services and systems.

The organizational knowledge creation theory they developed is based on the possibility of categorizing cognitive resources in terms of the following two essential dimensions:

- the *epistemological* dimension, which makes it possible to distinguish between explicit and tacit knowledge[1] (Arrow, 1962; Gelwick, 1977; Polanyi, 1966, 1985). *Explicit knowledge* can be expressed, codified and easily transferred between different people through formal and systematic languages. *Tacit* (or implicit) *knowledge*, on the contrary, originates from personal experiences; it is difficult to formalize; and it resides exclusively in the minds of individuals[2] (personal insights, personal experiential

---

[1] See Chapter Five, Note 1.

[2] In this regard, "...not always the firm, though made up by thinking individuals, is able to emulate the cerebral structure of each of them...". Excessively emphasizing the "firm as a cognitive system" metaphor can therefore be misleading (Golinelli, 2000, pp. 50-51).

skills, etc.)[3], often at different levels than that of "full awareness". Since explicit knowledge is only "the tip of the firm's knowledge iceberg" (Figure 13), where the foundations are essentially "tacit events" (which are difficult to express and share)[4], the fulcrum of the entrepreneurial process of knowledge creation lies in the capacity to mobilize, convert and disseminate the tacit knowledge of individuals throughout the organization;

- the *ontological* dimension, which makes it possible to categorize knowledge in relation to the entities involved in its creation (individual knowledge, group knowledge, organizational knowledge, inter-organizational knowledge). The firm's knowledge creation process can be described as an interactive, looping and spiral shaped process moving away from the individual level and gradually expanding and rising through ever higher ontological levels, which involve increasingly broader interacting communities.

1.2 Organizational Knowledge Creation Pathways

The interactions between individuals (social interactions) set into motion processes of knowledge evolution along the epistemo-

---

[3] Tacit knowledge has a dual nature: it is both technical and cognitive. The technical dimension includes all the informal skills that make up the "technical know-how" necessary for a given operation. The cognitive dimension is the full set of beliefs and mental schemes that help a person to perceive the world and define it, and to imagine its possible developments. See Nonaka & Takeuchi (1995).

[4] Polanyi (1966; 1985) reached his definition of the tacit part of knowledge as a direct result of recognizing the role played by the *personality* of "knowing" subjects (understanding is a personal act that cannot be replaced by a formal operation; a person knows more than he/she is able to express). According to the knower subject-known object separation axiom, human beings (subjects) acquire knowledge through analyzing external objects. Polanyi makes an important contribution to overcoming this axiom, in that he stresses that human beings acquire knowledge through active interaction with the objects in the world.

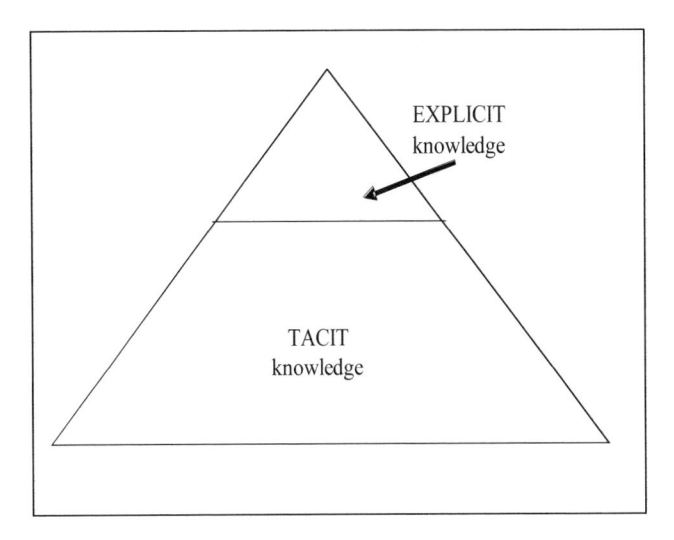

Figure 13. Polanyi's knowledge iceberg.

logical and ontological dimensions, thereby triggering a spiral of knowledge conversion processes (Nonaka & Takeuchi, 1995)[5].

---

[5] Nonaka and Takeuchi (1995) go beyond Simon's (1988) Cartesian rationalism, and make a crucial contribution by extending the interpretation of knowledge creation organizational dynamics, to include knowledge dimensions that had not previously been given their due weight, such as the "behavioral" dimension, introduced by Barnard (1938), and the "tacit" dimension discussed by Polanyi (1966).

Here are the main hypotheses on which Nonaka and Takeuchi's model is based:
- company knowledge is distributed among different individuals, and is mainly tacit in form;
- an individual's knowledge needs to be integrated. This integration requires the dissemination of knowledge among diverse subjects;
- knowledge integration, dissemination and recombination, generated by interactions between subjects, are a vital part of the creation of new knowledge;
- interaction between subjects must take place in an appropriate social context if the knowledge creation processes are to function effectively.

On the firm as a learning organization, also see (for example) Argyris & Schön (1998), Miggiani (1994), North (2005) and Tomassini (1993).

The *socialization* pathway consists of processes of tacit knowledge sharing among individuals, and generates new tacit knowledge through the social interaction arising therefrom. Since tacit knowledge cannot be codified, this cognitive path requires experience sharing, which in turn activates "fields of interaction" between those who possess a given experience and those who wish to acquire it. This may happen, for example, through recourse to on-the-job training practices[6] thus reproducing the apprentice-master craftsman relationship, in which the former learns from the latter through observation, imitation and practice. By way of "dialogue and group reflection" and methods of inductive and deductive reasoning, the *externalization* process makes it possible to convert tacit knowledge into new explicit knowledge, which takes the form of metaphor, analogy, concept, hypothesis and/or model. The complexity of the process is due to the fact that, in addition to being uncodified, implicit knowledge is closely linked to the mental models of individuals who possess it. The *combination* process makes it possible to produce new explicit knowledge by sorting, adding, combining and categorizing pre-existing explicit knowledge. Information and Communications Technologies facilitate this process by networking, and hence "systematizing" distinct corpuses of explicit knowledge. Finally *internalization* makes it possible to convert explicit knowledge into new tacit knowledge: applying explicit knowledge (codified in documents, manuals, etc.) to specific operational environments enables individuals to contextualize that knowledge, "to take possession of it", and to transform it into new implicit knowledge.

The nature of the new created knowledge depends on the way it is converted (Figure 14). Socialization produces *sympathetic* knowledge, that is to say, shared technical abilities and mental

---

[6] In order to be able to design a bread-making machine which would produce bread that was as good as that made by hand, the head of the software development division of the Japanese firm Matsushita Electric Industrial Company and several of his engineers decided to do "apprenticeships" in the best bakery in town so as to learn through direct experience how to make dough first hand (tacit knowledge learning). See Nonaka & Takeuchi (1995).

THE COGNITIVE INTERPRETATION

	To tacit knowledge	To explicit knowledge
From tacit knowledge	(Socialization): Sympathetic knowledge	(Externalization): Conceptual knowledge
From explicit knowledge	(Internalization): Operational knowledge	(Combination): Systemic knowledge

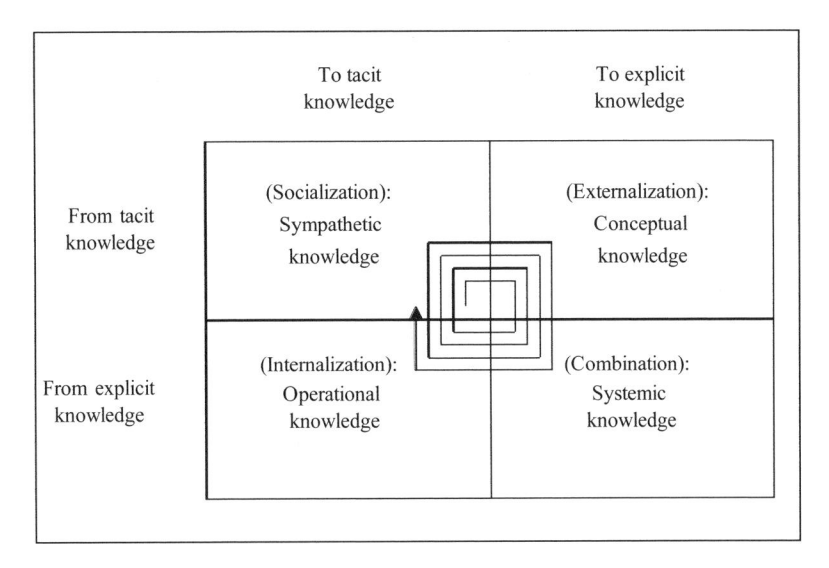

Figure 14. Knowledge conversion processes (Nonaka and Takeuchi, 1995).

schemes. Externalization creates *conceptual* knowledge (for example, the concept of a new product structure). Combination produces *systemic* knowledge (for example, the conceptual architecture of a new technology). Internalization produces *operational* knowledge (for example, project management innovative know-how).

Creating new knowledge can be viewed as a continuous and dynamic meta-process consisting of parallel iterations of the four knowledge conversion processes, the spiral shape of which shows the expansion of knowledge toward increasingly higher qualitative (i.e., *epistemological*) and *ontological* levels (from the individual to the organizational level, and to the inter-organizational level).

2. Meta-consulting Knowledge Conversion Pathways

The basic aim the of *meta-consulting*[7] intervention is the induction of new entrepreneurial knowledge, which both the client

---

[7] See Chapter Five.

and the consultant can exploit in the future, after the consulting project has been completed. I speak of "induction", rather than "transfer" of knowledge because the client and the consultant learn by implementing new knowledge creation cooperative processes and by connecting that knowledge to their own starting cognitive structures rather than by only acquiring new knowledge (which is codified to a greater or lesser degree). These processes are subjective by definition, and cannot be "taught". They can however be stimulated (induced) by the specific attitudes and conduct of the parties in the consulting relationship (discussion, explanation, recovery of previous experiences, active participation, etc.).

By making use of the conceptual categories developed by Nonaka and Takeuchi and by externalizing the implicit knowledge acquired through my own consulting experiences[8], I pro-

---

[8] Cognitive sciences have made great advances in the last decade or so, but even today we still know too little (and there is too little agreement) about how the human mind and brain function to be able to say that we have a complete theory of the mind which gives an exhaustive explanation of "knowledge". Of great interest, therefore is the work done by those who study knowledge from the viewpoint of psychology, of psychotherapeutic clinics, of sociology, and also of corporate organization and management; who are well aware how little we comprehend these matters today; and who endeavour to find new research inroads and to construct and test new interpretation models. I am of the opinion that we will not be helped, and may even be misled, by trying to elaborate complete theories on mind functioning that are based on the "reassuring" approaches of philosophical theories of the mind, or by adopting theories that seem "complete" merely, or mainly, because they are based on general concepts (such as Kelly's (1955) theory of personal constructs), and can therefore only theoretically be applied to all problematic contexts. A much better approach, I believe, is to accept the incompleteness of our existing knowledge and to work toward integrating this knowledge with that generated through the "consulting-clinic" experiences. Such knowledge is certainly difficult to generalize as it is necessarily based on individually observed cases; but it can provide heuristically significant indications, can highlight problems, pose questions, falsify existing theoretical models, and, consequently, stimulate the development of new models. In this sense, the consulting-clinic setting may be an excellent laboratory because its particular

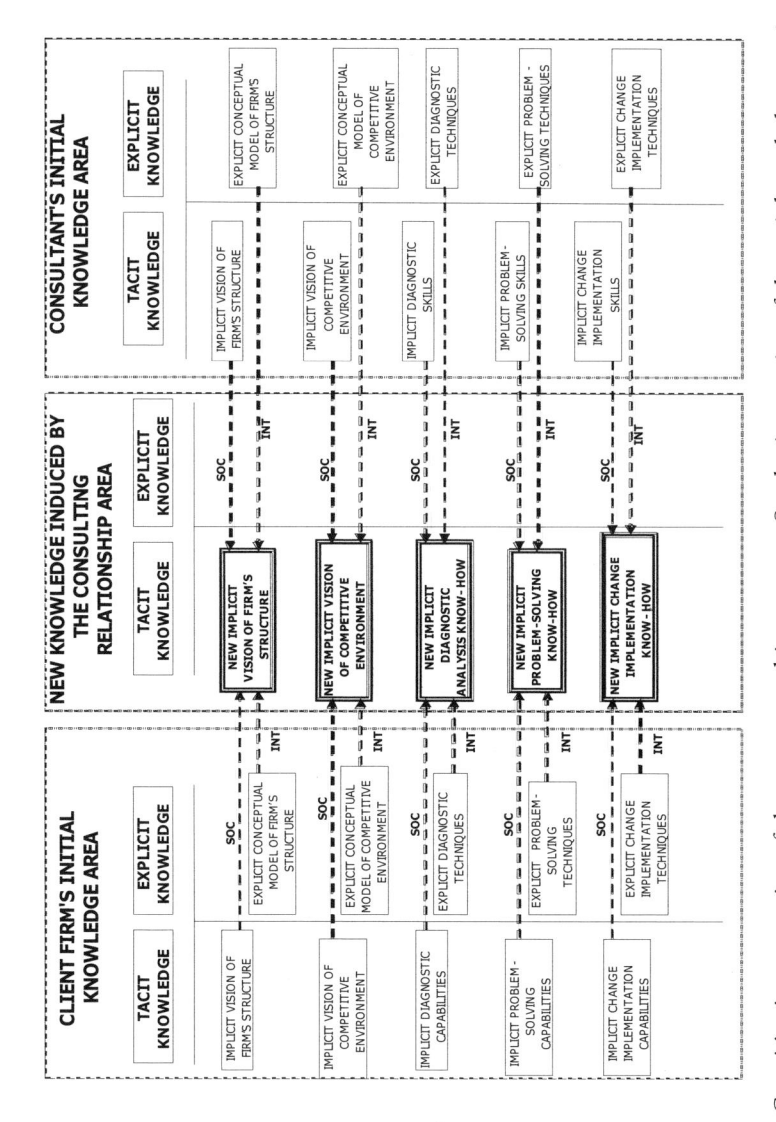

Figure 15. Cognitive interpretation of the meta-consulting process. Synthetic mapping of the tacit knowledge creation pathways: socialization (SOC) and internalization (INT).

pose in Figures 15 and 16 a possible conceptual mapping of the essential pathways through which the knowledge generation power of "high knowledge creation potential" consulting[9] can be expressed by following the *meta-consulting* approach[10].

Through *socialization* pathways, new tacit knowledge is induced by face-to-face interaction and by the subsequent informal sharing (and integration) of the pre-existing tacit knowledge owned by the two parties in the consulting relationship. Through active participation in the consulting experience, the client and the consultant submit their own initial tacit knowledge to a critical "justification" process based on direct and mutual comparison. This knowledge is "unfrozen" and, in the event of "non-confirmation", is renewed and converted into *new implicit knowledge*. Mutual direct observation, comparing different viewpoints, sharing and synchronizing experiences, insights and mental models, make it possible for both the client and the consultant:

a. to renew their own pre-existing *implicit visions of the firm's structure* (or functional portions of it) and *of the competitive environment*. For example, by sharing and comparing differing mental patterns, the client and the

---

characteristics allow in-depth study and close observation of cognitive dynamics to a much greater extent than is possible in abstract contexts and/or by observing "from the outside".

[9] See Chapter One.

[10] To study the wide spectrum of the knowledge creation processes involved in the consulting relationship, we need a clear definition of the "client" (Lundberg, 2002) and of the "consultant" as recognizable units of analysis. In this book, I manly take the client to be the firm's top management (or the entrepreneur), and the consultant to be the person in charge of carrying out the consulting intervention. This approach has been adopted also by Czerniawska (2002a) and by Linnarson & Werr (2002).

The proposed conceptual mapping of the knowledge creation pathways that can be activated through management meta-consulting interventions was first presented in October 2007 at the 7th Global Conference on Business & Economics (see Ciampi, 2007). See also Ciampi (in press-a; in press-b; in press-c).

consultant can cooperatively develop new ways of intuitively interpreting (and "seeing") the essential (qualitative and quantitative) features of the firm's structure, and new ways of interpreting (and "seeing") the relationship between the firm and its clients, the firm and its competitors, etc.;

b. to renew their own *implicit diagnostic, problem solving, and change implementation skills and capabilities.* By socializing their own pre-existing diagnostic-type implicit abilities, the client and the consultant can, for example, gain new intuitive abilities to sense the cause-effect relationships among the explanatory variables of entrepreneurial problems referring to a certain functional area (for example, the marketing area) and to intuitively distinguish, in the full set of involved variables, the "relatively primary" variables from the "relatively secondary" ones.

The entrepreneurial knowledge creation potential of socialization pathways that can be activated through meta-consulting interventions was very clearly perceived and expressed by one of the partners of a large-sized consultancy firm, which is a global leader in the strategy consulting field, who had the following to say:

> Classroom training was banished from our company over 10 years ago. Anyone wishing to work with us had to have learnt the basics of general management at business schools. However that knowledge is not sufficient. We attribute considerable weight to the mental flexibility of our collaborators, their humility, their determination and ability to learn from experience. Working "shoulder to shoulder" with more expert colleagues, and above all with clients on concrete consulting projects, makes it possible to learn, fine-tune, improve and develop one's own consulting skills, and it particularly enables development of the most important ability required of management consultants: the capacity to challenge their own mental patterns every time or, to put it another way, it teaches one to learn from experience. Our clients often do not realize it, but the value created by every consulting project gives us at least three times more than we charge them in fees. The entrepreneur knows his business

better than anyone else, and his company differs from every other company. Becoming totally immersed in this knowledge and in this diversity enables us to build up unique cognitive value, which none of our competitors will be able to imitate.

By applying their own explicit knowledge (diagnostic, problem solving and change implementation methods and techniques; conceptual models for interpreting the firm's structure and the competitive environment) to the specific context of the consulting intervention, both clients and consultants convert that knowledge into new tacit knowledge (*internalization* pathways) specific to the client's business context[11]. This is a very arduous cognitive path as it requires both parties to shun any temptation to merely replace the client's "existing practices" with the "best practices" (mainly explicit knowledge) which form part of the consultant's cognitive background, and instead to engage themselves in an intense activity of contextualization of that knowledge (by adapting it, changing it, redefining it, etc.) to the specific (business, competition, etc.) field with which the consulting intervention has to deal. For example, by experimenting with the application of their own codified techniques for entrepreneurial problem diagnosis to the specific client business context, consultants develop *new implicit diagnostic know-how* (uncodified skills and abilities) that is appropriate for defining the specific entrepreneurial problem, for discovering its causes, and for identifying the client firm's capabilities that can be used to solve it. The direct experiential sharing of this knowledge conversion process also makes it possible for clients to assimilate this new tacit knowledge, while at the same time

---

[11] Turning explicit knowledge ("general knowledge") into tacit knowledge ("idiosyncratic experience") is an essential and critical part of the consulting intervention, as has been shown by, among others, Sarvary (1999, p. 101): "There is no KM system that can account for the idiosyncrasies of a particular business situation". Consequently, even if a consulting firm has an efficient Knowledge Management system that can collect, update, synthesize and catalog the best practices, "if it is misused by incompetent people, it can lead to a disaster".

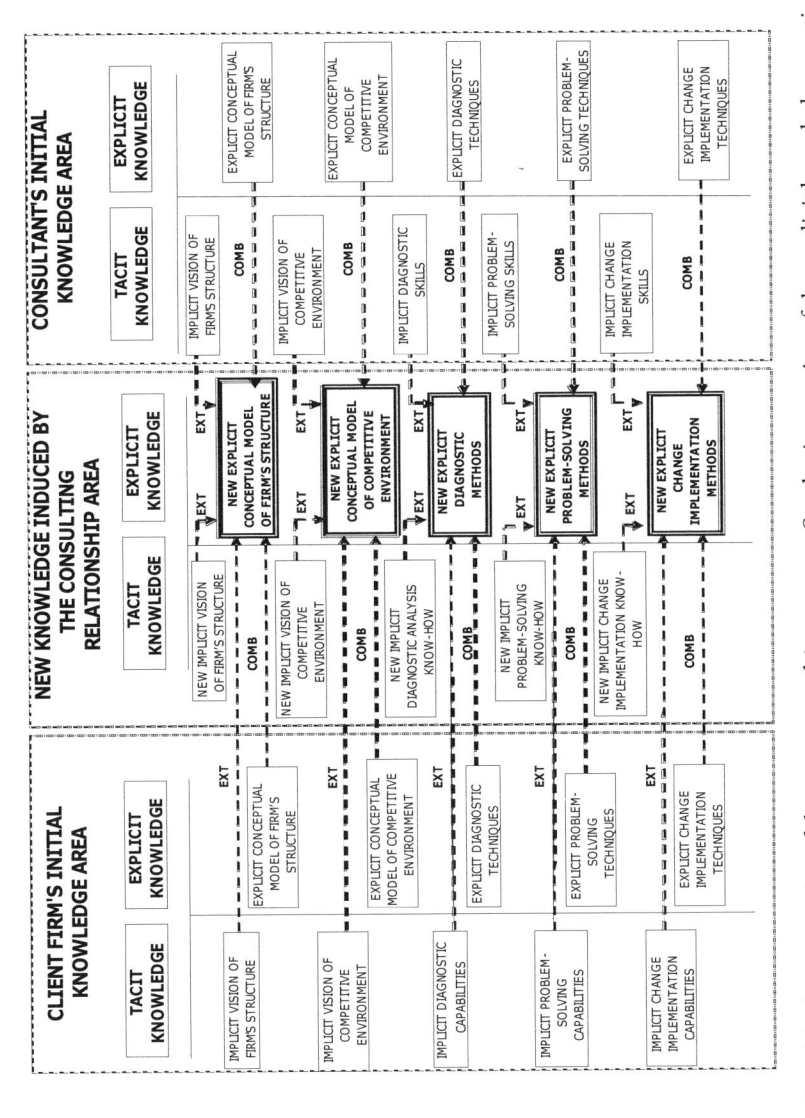

Figure 16. Cognitive interpretation of the meta-consulting process. Synthetic mapping of the explicit knowledge creation pathways: externalization (EXT) and combination (COMB).

subjecting their own pre-existing explicit diagnostic methods to critical justification, unfreezing, and renewal.

Through *externalization* pathways, the client and the consultant cooperatively convert their own tacit knowledge (both that pre-existing and the new knowledge generated through the consulting process) by translating perceptions, insights and experiences into explicit forms. Through these pathways, *new conceptual patterns and models* are created which, being explicit, are easily transmissible (to different levels of the organizational structure) through codified languages, and are also reusable in the future should the need arise. As new process (i.e., implicit) knowledge emerges that proves to work better than pre-existing knowledge (new tacit knowledge "which is shown to be true"), client-consultant social interaction shifts to the plane of a shared reflection, which, through the integrated use of inductive, deductive and abductive reasoning (metaphors and analogies[12]), aims to translate implicit knowledge into words, phrases and in the ultimate analysis, into explicit (formalized and codified) conceptual models. For example, from the initial phases of the consulting process, both client and consultant share the activity of codifying the client's initial implicit mental schemes for perceiving the qualitative and quantitative features of the firm's structure (*the client's initial implicit vision of the firm's structure*), thus making it possible to subject those schemes to critical justification and unfreezing processes (which will be fully implemented through successive internalization and socialization dynamics). Furthermore, during the whole consulting process, both client and consultant jointly endeavor to make explicit and codify the new tacit knowledge which emerges in the diagnostic phase (*implicit diagnostic analysis know-how*), in the therapeutic planning phase (*implicit problem-solving know-how*), and in the solution implementation phase (*implicit change implementation know-how*). This enables both parties to codify and learn *new explicit knowledge* (*models,*

---

[12] On the role of metaphors in the consultancy process, see, for example, Atkin & Perren (2000).

techniques, instruments and methods), which can be exploited in the future, once the consulting process is concluded.

Finally, through *combination* pathways the client and the consultant *integrate the new explicit knowledge* (which has been generated through the consulting process) *into their own pre-existing explicit conceptual systems.* There is a high level of knowledge creation potential in the combination pathway, even when the consulting intervention deals with partial areas of the client firm's structure (for example, a given business segment, or a given functional area). In these cases, in fact, the combination of new explicit "medium-range" knowledge with more general pre-existing concepts (for example, the explicit corporate vision) allows the older concepts to be enriched with new meanings. The creative use of ICT networks and hypertext information databases facilitates the combination pathway and helps both the client and the consultant to refreeze the new conceptual models and the new techniques that have been developed.

> Our best practices for designing and implementing management control systems have reached levels of excellence, particularly the ones that can be used by companies in the manufacturing and banking industries. I think they are the best in Europe. This has helped us to earn an excellent reputation, but our work remains extremely difficult. In fact, each new commission we receive entails immersing our logical, mathematical and statistical models into a specific corporate context and making them work in the best way possible in relation to each client company's specific [*present and future*] needs. To do this, we need the active cooperation of the client company's management. It is precisely thanks to this collaboration that we realize that our systems are failing to take account of important business interpretation keys, or that they possess potentialities which we had never previously realized. We offer our system to the client as the best available on the market (and we believe this to be true), but we have learned that in the course of every consulting intervention the main focus of our attention must be on seeking both the shortcomings and the latent potential of our systems and of their component modules [*consequently generating new implicit knowledge through* INTERNALIZATION]. The result is that almost all our consulting interventions lead us to modify (sometimes also to add) one or more modules [*thus EXTERNALIZING the new implicit knowledge*

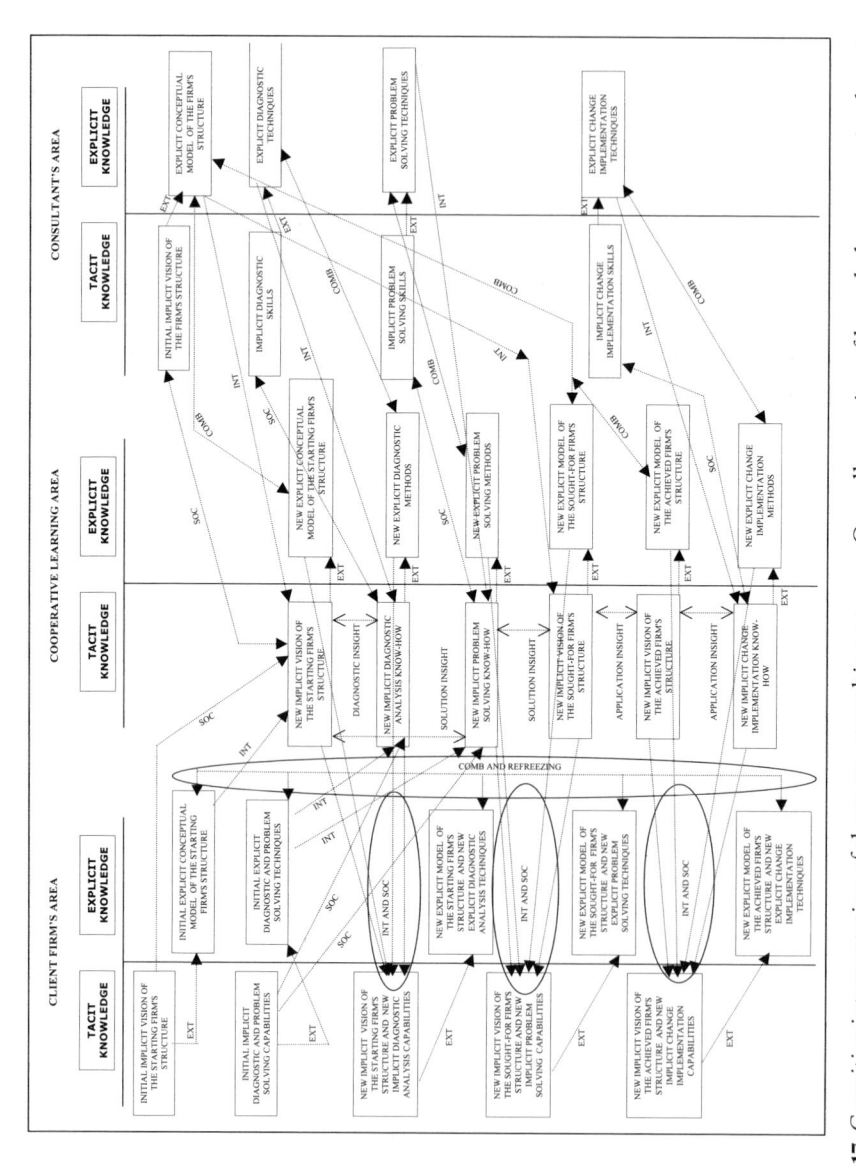

Figure 17. Cognitive interpretation of the meta-consulting process. Overall mapping of knowledge conversion learning processes: socialization (SOC), internalization (INT), externalization (EXT) and combination (COMB).

acquired during the consulting intervention], and some of the relationships which enable the various modules to function as a system [*hence RECOMBINING the new explicit knowledge generated through the consulting process*].

Apart from my (italicized) comments, these are the words of a senior consultant working for a large consulting firm, a leader in Europe in the management control systems consultancy. They provide an excellent example of how new (implicit and explicit) knowledge can be created by activating knowledge internalization, externalization and combination consulting pathways.

Figure 17 provides an overall map of the main cognitive pathways along which the entrepreneurial knowledge creation potential of meta-consulting can be brought into play.

References

Aadne, J. H., Kleine, D., Mahnke, V., & Venzin, M. (1997). *In search of inspiration: How managers, consultants and academics interact while exploring business strategy concepts.* Discussion Paper n. 28. Institute of Management. St. Gallen, Switzerland.

Abrahamson, E. (1996). Management fashion. *Academy of Management Review, 21*(1), 254-285.

Abrahamson, E., & Fairchild, G. (1999). Management fashion: Lifecycles, triggers, and collective learning processes. *Administrative Science Quarterly, 44*(4), 708-740.

Abrahamson, E., & Fairchild, G. (2001). Knowledge industries and idea entrepreneurs. In C. B. Schoonoven & E. Romanelli (Eds.), *The entrepreneurship dynamic* (pp. 147-177). Stanford, CA: Stanford University Press.

Abrahamson, E., & Ginsberg, A. (1991). Champions of change and strategic shifts: The role of internal and external change advocates. *Journal of Management Studies 28*(2), 173-190.

Ackenhusen, M., & Ghoshal, S. (1992). *Andersen Consulting: Entering the business of business integration.* Fontainbleau, France: Insead.

Adamson, I. (2000). Management consultant meets a potential client for the first time: The pre-entry phase of consultancy in SMEs and the issues of qualitative research methodology. *Qualitative Market Research: An International Journal, 3*(1), 17-26.

Ahmed, P. K., Lim, K. K., & Loh, A. Y. E. (2002). *Learning through knowledge management.* Woburn, MA: Butterworth Heinemann.

Aiello, G. M. (1995). *Consulenza di direzione e creazione di conoscenza.* Padua, Italy: Cedam.
Aiello, G. M. (1996). *Competizione e sviluppo delle imprese di consulenza.* Padua, Italy: Cedam.
Alavi, M., & Leidner, D. E. (2001). Knowledge management and knowledge management systems: Conceptual foundations and research issues. *MIS Quarterly, 25*(1), 107-136.
Alle, V. (2003). Knowledge networks and communities of practice. *Journal of the Organization Development Network, 32*(4), 45-61.
Allen, J., & David, D. (1992). Assessing some determinant effects of ethical consulting behaviour: The case of personal and professional values. *Journal of Business Ethics, 12*(6), 449-458.
Alvarez, J. L. (Ed.) (1998a). *The diffusion and consumption of business knowledge.* London, UK: Macmillan Press.
Alvarez, J. L. (1998b). The sociological tradition and the spread of institutionalization of knowledge for action. In J. L. Alvarez (Ed.), *The diffusion and consumption of business knowledge* (pp. 13-57). London, UK: Macmillan Press.
Alvesson, M. (1995). *Management of knowledge intensive companies.* Berlin, Germany: Walter de Gruyter.
Alvesson, M., & Karreman, D. (2001). Odd couple: Making sense of the curious concept of knowledge management. *Journal of Management Studies, 38*(7), 995-1118.
Ambler, A. R. (2006). How do you view your role as consultant? *Consulting to Management, 17*(2), 53-54.
Anand, N., Gardner, H. K., & Morris, T. (2007). Knowledge-based innovation: Emergence and embedding of new practice areas in management consulting firms. *Academy of Management Journal, 50*(2), 406-428.
Anonymous (1995). Rain making: The professional's guide to attracting new clients. *Journal of Management Consulting, 8*(3), 65.
Anonymous (1996). Confessions of an ex-consultant. *Fortune, 134*(7), 106-112.
Apostolou, D, & Mentzas, G. (1999a). Managing corporate knowledge: A comparative analysis of experiences in con-

sulting firms (Part 1). *Knowledge and Process Management*, 6(3), 129-138.

Apostolou, & D, Mentzas, G. (1999b). Managing corporate knowledge: A comparative analysis of experiences in consulting firms (Part 2). *Knowledge and Process Management*, 6(4), 238-254.

Arcari, A. (1991). *Economia delle imprese di servizi professionali.* Milan, Italy: Egea.

Argyris, C. (1961) Explorations in consulting-client relationships. *Human Organization*, 20(3), 121-133.

Argyris, C., & Schon, D. A. (1978). *Organizational learning: A theory of action perspective.* Reading, MA: Addison-Wesley.

Argyris, C., & Schon, D. A. (1998). *Apprendimento organizzativo: Teoria, metodo e pratiche.* Milan, Italy: Guerini e Associati.

Armbrüster, T. (2004). Rationality and its symbols: Signaling effects and subjectification in management consulting. *Journal of Management Studies*, 41(8), 1247-1269.

Armbrüster, T. (2006). *The economics and sociology of management consulting.* Cambridge, MA: Cambridge University Press.

Armbrüster, T., & Kipping, M. (2003). Strategy consulting at the crossroads: Technical change and shifting market conditions for top-level advice. *International Studies of Management & Organization*, 32(4), 19-42.

Armenakis, A. A., & Burdg, H. B. (1988). Consultation research: Contributions to practice and directions for improvement. *Journal of Management*, 14(2), 339-365.

Armstrong, T. R. (1993). Twenty-five lessons from twenty-five years of consulting to organizations and communities. *Organization Development Journal*, 11(3), 33-38.

Arrow, K. (1962). Economic welfare and the allocation of resources for invention. In Universities-National Bureau Committee for Economic Research (Ed.), *The rate and direction of inventive activity* (pp. 609-626). Cambridge, MA: Harvard Business School Press.

Ashford, M. (1999). *Con-tricks: The shadowy world of management consultancy and how to make it work for you.* New York, NY: Simon & Schuster.

Aspatore Books Staff (Ed.) (2005). *The art of consulting: Gaining loyalty, achieving profitability, & adding value as a consultant.* Boston, MA: Aspatore Books.

Assco (Ed.) (1996). *La consulenza di direzione e il suo mercato.* Turin, Italy: Isedi.

Atkin, R., & Perren, L. (2000). The role of metaphors in the strategic change consultancy process: The case of Sir John Harvey-Jones. *Strategic Change, 9*(5), 275-285.

Axelrod, E., Axelrod, R. H., Beedon, J., & Jacobs, R. W. (2006). Beat the odds and succeed in organizational change. *Consulting to Management, 17*(2), 6-9.

Azzariti, F., & Mazzon, P. (2005). *Il valore della conoscenza: Teoria e pratica del knowledge management prossimo e venturo.* Milan, Italy: Etas.

Baaij, M. G., Van den Bosch, F. A. J, & Volberda, H. W. (2005a) How knowledge accumulation has changed strategy consulting: Strategic options for established strategy consulting firms. *Strategic Change, 14*(1), 25-34.

Baaij, M. G., Van den Bosch, F. A. J., & Volberda, H. W. (2005b). The impact of management consulting firms on building and leveraging clients' competences. In R. Sanchez & A. Heene (Eds.), *Competence perspectives on managing inter-firm interactions - Advances in Applied Business Strategy - Vol. 8* (pp. 27-44). Oxford, UK: Elsevier.

Barcus, III, S. W., & Wilkinson, J. W (1995). *Handbook of management consulting services (2nd ed.).* New York, NY: McGraw-Hill.

Barnard, C. I. (1938). *The functions of the executive.* Cambridge, MA: Harvard University Press.

Barr, P. S., Huff, A. S., & Stimpert, J. L. (1992). Cognitive change, strategic action, and organizational renewal. *Strategic Management Journal, 13*(36), 15-36.

Becker, G. (1962). Investment in human capital: A theoretical analysis. *Journal of Political Economy, 70*(5), 9-49.

Becker, G. (1964). *Human capital: A theoretical and empirical analysis with special reference to education.* New York, NY: National Bureau of Economic Research.

Becker, G. (1976). *The economic approach to human behaviour.* Chicago, IL: University of Chicago Press.

Beckman, T. (1997). *A methodology for knowledge management.* Banff, Canada: International Association for Science and Technology for Development.

Beich, E. (1998). *The Business of consulting: The basics and beyond.* San Francisco, CA: Jossey-Bass/Pfeiffer.

Beich, E. (2001). *The consultant's quick start guide: An action plan for your first year in business.* San Francisco, CA: Jossey-Bass/Pfeiffer.

Beich, E., & Swindling, L. B. (1999). *The Consultant's legal guide.* San Francisco, CA: Jossey-Bass/Pfeiffer.

Bell, C. R. (1986). Entry is a critical phase in consulting. *Journal of Management Consulting, 3*(1), 4-9.

Bell, C. R., & Nadler, L. (Eds.) (1985). *Clients and consultants: Meeting and exceeding expectations.* Houston, TX:. Gulf Publishing Co.

Bellman, G. M. (1990). *The consultant's calling.* San Francisco, CA: Jossey-Bass/Pfeiffer.

Bennett, R. (1990). *Choosing and using management consultants.* London, UK: Kogan Page.

Bennett, R. J., & Smith, C. (2004). Spatial markets for consultancy to smes. *Tijdschrift voor Economische en Sociale Geografie, 95*(4), 359-374.

Bergholz, H., & Nickols, F. (2000a). The independent consultant as "equilateralist" (Part 1). *Consulting to Management, 11*(2), 26-27.

Bergholz, H., & Nickols, F. (2000b). The independent consultant as "equilateralist" (Part 2). *Consulting to Management, 11*(3), 23-24.

Bergholz, H., & Nickols, F. (2001). The independent consultant as "equilateralist" (Part 3). *Consulting to Management, 12*(1), 37-38.

Bergholz, H., Nickols, F. (2003). Protect your practice proactively! *Consulting to Management, 14*(2), 12-13.

Berini, G., & Guida, G. (2000). *Ingegneria della conoscenza. Strumenti per innovare e per competere.* Milan, Italy: Egea.

Berry, J. (2006). M&A-The next big thing? *Consulting to Management, 17*(2), 30-31.

Berthon, A., Child, J., Dierkes, M., & Nonaka, I. (Eds.). (2001). *Handbook of organizational learning & knowledge.* Oxford, UK: Oxford University Press.

Bessant, J., & Rush, H. (1995). Building bridges for innovation: The role of consultants in technology transfer. *Research Policy, 24*(1), 97-114.

Bettiol, C. (2005). *On intellectual capital: Exogenous and endogenous complexity.* Paper prepared for 4th International Critical Management Studies Conference, Cambridge, MA.

Bianchini, M. (1999). *Le radici del knowledge management: Il modello delle competenze.* Milan, Italy: Etas.

Biech, E. (1998). *The business of consulting.* San Francisco, CA: Jossey-Bass/Pfeiffer.

Biech, E. (2002). *Consulting.* San Francisco, CA: Jossey-Bass/Pfeiffer.

Biech, E., & Swindling, L. B. (2000). *The consultant's legal guide.* San Francisco, CA: Jossey-Bass/Pfeiffer.

Biswas, S., & Twitchell, D. (2002). *Management consulting: A complete guide to the industry (2nd ed.).* New York, NY: Wiley.

Blacker, F. (1995). Knowledge, knowledge work and organizations: An overview and interpretation. *Organization Studies, 16*(6), 1021-1046.

Block, P. (1993). *La consulenza perfetta.* Milan (Italy): FrancoAngeli.

Block, P. (2000). *Flawless consulting (2nd ed.).* San Francisco, CA: Jossey-Bass/Pfeiffer.

Bloom, F. B. (1992). The psychology of rainmaking. *Journal of Management Consulting, 7*(2), 50-54.

Bly, R. W. (1998). *The six-figure consultant.* Chicago, IL: Upstart.

Bobrow, E. E (1986). Grand strategies for marketing small consultants. *Journal of Management Consulting, 3*(1), 37-43.

Bobrow, E. E (1994). Personal goals: The base for goals as a consultant. *Journal of Management Consulting, 8*(1), 15-18.

Bobrow, E. E (1997a). Developing new consulting products. *Journal of Management Consulting, 9*(3), 56-59.

Bobrow, E. E (1997b). Don't be the shoemaker without shoes. *Journal of Management Consulting*, 9(4), 38-40.

Bobrow, E. E (1998a). How to be a learning individual. *Journal of Management Consulting*, 10(1), 43-45.

Bobrow, E. E (1998b). Poof! You're a consultant. *Journal of Management Consulting*, 10(2), 41-43.

Bobrow, E. E (1999). Consultants of the world unite! *Journal of Management Consulting*, 10(3), 61-64.

Bonnet, M., Moore, R., Savall, H., & Zardet, V. (2001). A system-wide, integrated methodology for intervening in organizations: The ISEOR approach. In A. F. Buono (Ed.), *Current trends in management consulting* (pp. 105-125). Greenwich, CT: Information Age Publishing.

Bou, E., & Sauquet, A. (2005). Knowing in the consultancy firm. In A. F. Buono & F. Poulfelt (Eds.), *Challenges and issues in knowledge management* (pp. 69-106). Greenwich, CT: Information Age Publishing.

Bower, M. (1997). *The will to lead. Boston.* MA: Harvard Business School Press.

Bowers, W. B., & Degler, W. P. (1999). Engaging engagements. *Journal of Management Consulting*, 10(4), 23-28.

Brelsford, H. (2003). *SMB consulting best practices.* Norwood, MA: Hara Publishing Group.

Brondoni, S. M. (1978). *Le agenzie di pubblicità: Evoluzione funzionale e problemi di gestione.* Milan, Italy: Giuffrè.

Brondoni, S. M. (2002a). Ouverture de "Market-space management". *Symphonya. Emerging Issues in Management*, www.unimib.it/symphonya, 2(1).

Brondoni, S. M. (2002b). Global markets and market-space competition. *Symphonya. Emerging Issues in Management*, www.unimib.it/symphonya, 2(1).

Brondoni, S. M. (2007). Market-driven management ed economia d'impresa globale. In S. M. Brondoni (Ed.), *Market-driven management, concorrenza e mercati globali* (pp. 19-63). Turin, Italy: G. Giappichelli.

Brotheridge, C., & Power, J. (2007). Spending consulting dollars wisely: A guide for management. *Team Performance Management*, 13(1/2), 53-56.

Brown, J. S., & Duguit P. (2001). Knowledge and organization: A social-practice perspective. *Organization Science, 12*(2), 198-213.

Bukh, P. N., & Mouritsen, J. (2005). Managing organizational knowledge networks in a professional firm: Interrelating knowledge management and intellectual capital. In A. F. Buono & F. Poulfelt (Eds.), *Challenges and issues in knowledge management* (pp. 3-21). Greenwich, CT: Information Age Publishing.

Buono, A. F. (Ed.) (2001). *Current trends in management consulting.* Greenwich, CT: Information Age Publishing.

Buono, A. F. (Ed.) (2002). *Developing knowledge and value in management consulting.* Greenwich, CT: Information Age Publishing.

Buono, A. F. (Ed.) (2003). *Enhancing inter-firm networks and interorganizational strategies.* Greenwich, CT: Information Age Publishing.

Buono, A. F. (Ed.) (2004). *Creative consulting: Innovative perspectives on management consulting.* Greenwich, CT: Information Age Publishing.

Buono, A. F., & Kerber, K. W (2005). Rethinking organizational change: Reframing in the challenge of change management. *Organization Development Journal, 23*(3), 23-38.

Buono, A. F., & Poulfelt, F. (2005a). Introduction. In A. F. Buono, & F. Poulfelt (Eds.), *Challenges and issues in knowledge management* (pp. ix-xxiv). Greenwich, CT: Information Age Publishing.

Buono, A. F., & Poulfelt, F. (Eds.) (2005b). *Challenges and issues in knowledge management.* Greenwich, CT: Information Age Publishing.

Buono, A. F., & Savall, H. (Eds.) (2007). *Socio-economic intervention in organizations: The intervener-researcher and the seam approach to organizational analysis.* Charlotte, North Carolina: Information Age Publishing.

Cafferata, R. (1998). La consulenza aziendale: Contenuto ed evoluzione. *Il giornale dei Dottori Commercialisti, Issue 5.*

Cambell, T. (2002). Once we had professionals. *Journal of Management Consulting, 13*(3), 16-17.

Canback, S. (1998). The Logic of Management Consulting (Part one). *Journal of Management Consulting, 10*(2), 3-11.

Canback, S. (1999). The Logic of Management Consulting (Part two). *Journal of Management Consulting, 10*(3), 3-12.

Carucci, R. A., & Tetenbaum, T. J. (1999). *The value-creating consultant: How to build and sustain lasting client relationships.* New York, NY: Amacom.

Chapin Jr, J. N. (2006). Are you prepared for the consultant's nightmare? *Consulting to Management, 17*(1), 7-8.

Christensen, P. R., & Klyver, K. (2006).Management consultancy in small firms: How does interaction work? *Journal of Small Business and Enterprise Development, 13*(3), 299-313

Chung, Q. B., Luo, W., & Wagner, W. P. (2006). Strategic alliance of small firms in knowledge industries: A management consulting perspective. *Business Process Management Journal, 12*(2), 206-233.

Ciampi, F. (2004). *Fondamenti di economia e gestione delle imprese.* Florence, Italy: Firenze University Press.

Ciampi, F. (2007). *Knowledge creation through management consulting.* Paper presented at the 7th Global Conference on Business & Economics, Rome, Italy (October).

Ciampi, F. (in press-a). Management consulting and knowledge creation. *Symphonya. Emerging Issues in Management*, www.unimib.it/symphonya.

Ciampi, F. (in press-b). Exploring knowledge creation pathways in advanced management consulting. In A. F. Buono (Ed.), *Emerging trends and issues in management consulting.* Charlotte, NC: Information Age Publishing.

Ciampi, F. (in press-c). Defining management consulting and exploring its knowledge creation potential. *International Journal of Business & Economics.*

Ciappei, C. (1991). *Autonomia e assetti d'impresa.* Turin, Italy: Giappichelli.

Cittadini, G. (Ed.) (2004). *Capitale umano. La ricchezza dell'Europa.* Milan, Italy: Guerini e Associati.

Clark K. B., Hayes, R. H., & Wheelwright, S. C. (1988). *Dynamic manufacturing: Creating the learning organization.* New York, NY: The Free Press.

Clark, T. (1995). *Managing consultants. Consultancy as the management of impressions.* Birmingham, UK: Open University Press.

Clark, T., & Fincham, R. (Eds.) (2002). *Critical consulting: New perspectives on the management advice industry.* Malden, MA: Blackwell Publishers.

Clark, T., & Salaman, G. (1996). The management guru as organizational witchdoctor. *Organization, 3*(1), 85-107.

Clark, T., & Salaman, G. (1998a). Telling tales: Management gurus' narratives and the construction of managerial identity. *Journal of Management Studies, 35*(2), 137-161.

Clark, T., & Salaman, G. (1998b). Creating the 'right' impression: Towards a dramaturgy of management consulting. *Services Industries Journal, 18*(1), 18-38.

Clive, R., & David, O. (1991). *Management consultancy: The inside story.* London, UK: Mercury Books.

Cockman, P., Evans, B., & Reynolds, P. (1996). *Client-centered consulting: Getting your expertise used when you're not in charge.* New York, NY: McGraw Hill.

Cody, T. G. (1986). *Management consulting: A game without chips.* New York, NY: Kennedy Pubblications.

Cohen, K. P., & Low, J. (2002). *Invisible advantage: How intangibles are driving business performance.* Cambridge, MA: Perseus Group.

Cohen, W. A. (1989). *Il consulente di successo.* Milano, Italy: Sperling & Kupfer.

Cohen, W. A. (1991). *How to make it big as a consultant* (2nd ed.). New York, NY: Amacom.

Cohen, W. M., & Levinthal, D. A. (1990). Absorptive capacity: A new perspective on learning and innovation. *Administrative Science Quarterly, 35*(1), 128-152.

Connell, C., Klein, J. H., Loebbecke, C., & Powell, P. (2001). Towards a knowledge management consultation system. *Knowledge and Process Management, 8*(1), 48-54.

Connor, D., & Davidson, J. (1990). *Marketing your consulting and professional services.* New York, NY: Wiley.

Cook, M. F. (1996). *Consulting on the side.* New York, NY: Wiley.

Cook, S. D., & Yanow D. (1993). Culture and organizational learning. *Journal of Management Inquiry*, 2(4), 373-390.

Cope, M. (2003). *The seven CS of consulting: The definitive guide to the consulting process (3nd ed.).* Englewood Cliffs, NJ: Prentice-Hall.

Corbetta, G. (2000). *La consulenza di direzione. Profili economico-aziendali.* Milan, Italy: Egea.

Corbetta G., & Mazzola P. (1999). L'evoluzione della consulenza strategica in Italia: esperienze a confronto (1). *Economia & Management, Issue 5*, 33-38.

Corbetta G., & Mazzola P. (2000a). L'evoluzione della consulenza strategica in Italia: esperienze a confronto (2). *Economia & Management, Issue 2*, 31-36.

Corbetta G., & Mazzola P. (2000b). L'evoluzione della consulenza strategica in Italia: esperienze a confronto (3). *Economia & Management, Issue 5*, 36-40.

Corcoran, J., & McLean, F. (1998). The selection of management consultants: How are government dealing with this difficult decision? An exploratory study. *International Journal of Public Sector Management* 11(1), 37-54.

Cortada, J. W., & Woods, J. A. (1999). *The knowledge management yearbook 1999-2000.* Boston, MA: Butterworth-Heinemann.

Covin, T. J., & Fisher, T. V. (1991). Consultant and client must work together. *Journal of Management Consulting* 6(4), 11-19.

Cowan, R., David, P. A., & Foray, D. (2000). The explicit economics of knowledge codification and tacitness. *Industrial and Corporate Change*, 9(2), 211-53.

Cox, C. A. (1985). The art of prying out information. *Journal of Management Consulting*, 2(2), 22-25.

Cravera, A., Maglione, M., & Ruggeri R. (2001). *La valutazione del capitale intellettuale.* Milan, Italy: Il Sole 24 ore.

Creplet, F., Dupouet, O., Kerna, F., Mehmanpazir, B., & Munier, F. (2001). Consultants and experts in management consulting firms. *Research Policy*, 30(9), 1517–1535.

Crucini, C. (2002). Knowledge management at the country level: A large consulting firm in Italy. In L. Engwall & M. Kipping

(Eds.), *Management consulting: Emergence and dynamics of a knowledge industry* (pp. 109-128). Oxford, UK: Oxford University Press.

Cuneo, G. (1996). *Il successo degli altri*. Milan, Italy: Bain, Cuneo e Associati.

Cveljo, K. (1993). *Management Consulting*. Metuchen, NJ: Scarecrow Press.

Czerniawska, F. (2002a). *Management consulting: What next?* London, UK: Palgrave.

Czerniawska, F. (2002b). *Value-Based Consulting*. London, UK: Palgrave.

Czerniawska, F. (2005). Will Consulting Go Online? In L. Greiner & F. Poulfelt (Eds.), *Handbook of management consulting: The contemporary consultant-insight from world experts* (pp. 329-343). Mason, OH: Thompson South Western.

Czerniawska, F. (2006a). Are we placing too much faith in trust? *Consulting to Management, 17*(1), 3-4.

Czerniawska, F. (2006b). Consultant: good. Consulting firm: bad. *Consulting to Management, 17*(2), 3-5.

Czerniawska, F. (2007). *The trusted firm: How consulting firms build successful client relationships*. New York, NY: Wiley.

Czerniawska, F., & May, P. (2006). *Management consulting in practice: A casebook of international best practice*. London, UK: Kogan Page.

Daft, R. L. (2001). *Organizzazione aziendale*. Milan, Italy: Apogeo.

Darr, E. D., Argote, L., & Epple, D. (1995). The acquisition, transfer, and depreciation of knowledge in service organizations: Productivity in franchises. *Management Science, 41*(11), 1750-1762.

Davenport, T. H., & Prusak, L. (1998). *Working knowledge. How organizations manage what they know*. Boston, MA: Harvard Press.

Davenport, T. H., & Prusak, L. (2000). *Il sapere al lavoro: Come le imprese possono generare, codificare e trasferire conoscenza*. Milan, Italy: Etas.

Davenport, T. H., & Prusak, L. (2005). Knowledge management in consulting. In L. Greiner & F. Poulfelt (Eds.), *Handbook of management consulting. The contemporary consultant: Insight from world experts* (pp. 305-326). Mason, OH: Thompson South Western.

Dawes, P. L., Lee, D. Y., & Midgley, D. (2007). Organizational learning in high-technology purchase situations: The antecedents and consequences of the participation of external IT consultants. *Industrial Marketing Management, 36*(3), 285-299.

Dawson, R. (2005). *Developing knowledge-based client relationships: Leadership in professional services (2nd ed.).* London, UK: Elsewir.

De Bono, E. (1977). *Lateral thinking: A textbook of creativity.* Harmondsworth, UK: Penguin Books.

De Bono, E. (1991). *Sei cappelli per pensare: Un manuale pratico per ragionare con creatività ed efficienza.* Milan, Italy: Rizzoli.

De Burgundy, J. (1998). Management consultancy: a modern folly? *Management Decision, 36*(3), 204-205.

De Haan, E. (2006). *Fearless consulting: Temptations, risks and limits of the profession.* Hoboken, NJ: Wiley.

De Long, D. W., & Fahey, L. (2000). Diagnosing cultural barriers to knowledge management. *Academy of Management Executive, 14*(4), 113-127.

Dean, J. (1938). The place of management counsel in business. *Harvard Business Review, 16*(4), 451-465.

Dechant, K., Marsick, V., & Kasl, E. (1993). Toward a model of team learning. *Studies in Continuing Education, 15*(1), 1-14.

Docherty, P., Stjernberg, T., & Werr, A. (1997). The functions of methods of change in management consultancy. *Journal of Organizational Change Management, 10*(4), 288-307.

Dodgson, M. (1993). Organizational learning: A review of some literatures. *Organization Studies, 14*(3), 375-394.

Domsch, M. E., & Hristozova, E. (Eds.) (2006). *Human resource management in consulting firms.* Berlin, Germany: Springer-Verlag.

Dougherty, A. M. (1995). *Consultation: Practice and perspectives in school and community settings (2nd ed.).* Pacific Grove, CA: Brooks Cole Publishing.

Dowling, G. (1993). Buying professional services: A client's perspective. *Management, January/February*, 13-14.

Drucker, P. F. (1995). *Managing in a time of great change.* Oxford, UK: Butterworth Heinemann.

Duncan, R. B., & Weiss, A. (1979). Organizational learning: Implications for organizational design. In L. L. Cummings & B. M. Staw (Eds.), *Research in organizational behaviour* (pp. 75-123). Greenwich, CT: Jai Press.

Dunford, R. (2000). Key challenges in the search for the effective management of knowledge in management consulting firms. *Journal of Knowledge Management*, 4(4), 295-302.

Dwyer, A. F., & Harding, F. (1996). Using ideas to increase the marketability of your firm. *Journal of Management Consulting*, 9(2), 56-61.

Earl, M. J., & Scott, I. A. (1999). What is a chief knowledge officer? *Sloan Management Review*, 40(2), 29-38.

Easley, C., & Harding, C. (1999). Client vs. consultant. Fishbowl or foxhole? *Journal of Management Consulting* 10(4), 3-8.

Easterby, S. M. (2000). Organizational learning: Debate past, present and future. *Journal of Management Studies*, 37(6), 783-796.

Easterby, S. M., & Lyles, M. A. (Eds.) (2003). *Handbook of organization learning and knowledge management.* Oxford, Malden: Blackwell.

Eccles, R. G., Shapiro, E. C., & Soske, T. L. (1993). Consulting: Has the solution become part of the problem? *Sloan Management Review*, 34(4), 89-95.

Edersheim, E. H. (2004). *McKinsey's Marvin Bower: Vision, leadership, and the creation of management consulting.* New York, NY: Wiley.

Edvardsson, B. (1990). Management consulting towards a successful relationship. *International Journal of Service Industry Management*, 1(3), 4-19.

EIU (1993). *Research report: Choosing and using a management consultant (2nd ed.).* London, UK: The Economist Intelligence Unit.

Ejenäs, M., & Werr, A. (2005). Merging knowledge. In A. F. Buono & F. Poulfelt (Eds.), *Challenges and issues in knowledge management* (pp. 179-207). Greenwich, CT: Information Age Publishing.

Elkjaer, B., Flensburg, P., Mouritsen, J., & Willmot, H. (1991). The commodification of expertise: The case of system development consulting. *Accounting Management & Information*, 1(2), 139-156.

Empson, L., & Morris, T. (1998). Organization and expertise: An exploration of knowledge bases and the management of accounting and consulting firms. *Accounting, Organizations and Society*, 23(56), 609-624.

Engwall, L., Alvarez, J. L., Amdam, R. P., & Kipping, M. (2001). *The creation of European management practice: The final report.* Uppsala, Sweden: CEMP.

Engwall, L., & Eriksson, C. B. (1999). *Advising corporate superstars.* Paper presented at the 2nd International Conference on Management Consultancy Work, London, UK.

Engwall, L., & Kipping, M. (2002a). Introduction: Management consulting as a knowledge industry. In M. Kipping & L. Engwall (Eds.). *Management consulting: emergence and dynamics of a knowledge industry* (pp. 1-16). Oxford, UK: Oxford University Press.

Engwall, L., & Kipping, M. (Eds.) (2002b). *Management consulting: Emergence and dynamics of a knowledge industry.* Oxford, UK: Oxford University Press.

Engwall, L., & Sahlin-Andersson, K. (Eds.) (2002a). *The expansion of management knowledge: Carriers, flows, and sources.* Stanford, CA: Stanford University Press.

Engwall, L., & Sahlin-Andersson, K. (2002b). The dynamics of management knowledge expansion. In L. Engwall & K. Sahlin-Andersson (Eds.), *The expansion of management knowledge: Carriers, flows, and sources.* Stanford, CA: Stanford University Press.

Eppler, M. (2003). *Managing information quality: Increasing the value of information in knowledge-intensive products and processes.* Berlin, Germany: Springer.

Ernst, B, & Kieser, A. (2002). In search of explanations for the consulting explosion. In L. Engwall & K. Sahlin-Andersson

(Eds.), *The expansion of management knowledge: Carriers, flows, and sources* (pp. 47-73). Stanford, CA: Stanford University Press.

Ernst, B., & Kieser, A. (2003). *Why neither managers nor consultants need nor want systematic evaluations of consulting engagements.* Paper presented at the 63rd Annual Meeting of the Academy of Management Conference, Seattle, USA (August).

Evans, M., & Fincham, R. (1999). 'The consultants' offensive: Reengineering-From fad to technique. *New Technology, Work and Employment, 14*(1), 50-63.

Faliva, G., & Pennarola, F. (1992). *Storia della consulenza di direzione in Italia.* Milan, Italy: Edizione Olivares.

Faust, M. (2002). Consultancies as actors in knowledge arenas: Evidence from Germany. In M. Kipping & L. Engwall (Eds.). *Management consulting: Emergence and dynamics of a knowledge industry* (pp. 146-163). Oxford, UK: Oxford University Press.

Fazzi, R. (1982). *Il governo d'impresa (Volume I).* Milan, Italy: Giuffrè.

Fazzi, R. (1984). *Il governo d'impresa (Volume II).* Milan, Italy: Giuffrè.

FEACO (2005). *2005 Survey of the European management consultancy market.* Brussels, Belgium: European Federation of. Management Consulting Association.

Ferrandina, A. (2006). Consulenza direzionale alle imprese. *PMI, Issue 8*, 63-65.

Fincham, R. (1995). Business process reengineering and the commodification of management knowledge. *Journal of Marketing Management, 11*(7), 707-720.

Fincham, R. (1999a). The consultant-client relationship: Critical perspectives on the management of organizational change. *Journal of Management Studies, 36*(3), 331-351.

Fincham, R. (1999b). *Rhetorical narratives and the consultancy process.* Paper presented at the British Academy of Management Conference, Manchester, UK (September).

Fincham, R. (2002a). The agent's agent: Power, knowledge and uncertainty in management consultancy. *International Studies of Management and Organization, 32*(4), 67-86.

Fincham, R. (2002b) Knowledge work as occupational strategy: Comparing IT and management consulting. *New Technology, Work and Employment*, 21(1), 16-28.

Fincham, R., & Clark, T. (Eds.) (2002). *Critical consulting.* Oxford, UK: Blackwell Business.

Fincham, R., & Clark, T. (2003). Management consultancy: Issues, perspectives, and agendas. *International Studies of Management & Organization*, 32(4), 3-18.

Fiol, C. M., & Lyles, M. A. (1985). Organizational learning. *Academy of Management Review*, 10(4), 803-813.

Fischer, R., & Rabaut, M. (1992). A how-to guide: Working with a consultant. *Management Review*, 81(2), 52-55.

Fleming, S. C. (1989). Compatibility pays off. *Journal of Business Strategy*, 10(3), 4-7.

Folchini, E., Gaiarin, N., & Rinaldi, A. (2005). *Counseling per manager: Modelli, esperienze e metafore per gestire il cambiamento.* Milan, Italy: Guerini e Associati.

Fombrun, C. J., & Nevins, M. D. (2004). *The advice business: Essential tools and models for management consulting.* Upper Saddle River, NJ: Pearson/Prentice Hall.

Fontana, F., & Lorenzoni, G. (2004). *Il knowledge management.* Rome, Italy: Luiss University Press.

Fontana, M. (1988). Il rapporto consulente/committente: Brain, Grey-Hair o Procedure? *Sviluppo & Organizzazione, Issue 108.*

Ford, C. H. (1985). Developing a successful client consultant relationship. In C. R. Bell & L. Nadler (Eds.), *Clients and consultants: Meeting and exceeding expectations* (pp.8-21). Houston, TX: Gulf Publishing Co.

Foss, N. J. (1996). Knowledge-based approaches to the theory of the firm: Some critical comments. *Organizational Science*, 7(5), 470-476.

Fosstenløkken, S. M., Løwendahl, B. R., & Revang, Ø. (2003). Knowledge development through client interaction: A comparative study. *Organization Studies*, 24(6), 859-879.

Frankenhuis, J. (1977). How to get a good consultant. *Harvard Business Review*, 55(6), 133-139.

Freedman, R. (2000). *The IT consultant*. San Francisco, CA: Jossey-Bass.
Fridenson, P. (1994). La circulation internationale des modes managériales. In J. P. Bouilloud & B. P. Lecuyer (Eds.), *L'invention de la gestion. Histoire et pratiques* (pp. 81-89). Paris, France: L'Harmattan.
Fuchs, J. H. (1975). *Making the most of management consulting services*. New York, NY: Amacom.
Gable, G. (2003). Editorial preface: Consultants and knowledge management. *Journal of Global Information Management, 1*(3), I-IV.
Galford, R. M., Green, C. H., & Maister, D. H. (2000a). *The trusted advisor*. New York, NY: Free Press.
Galford, R. M., Green, C. H., & Maister, D. H. (2000b). What is a trusted advisor? *Consulting to Management, 11*(3), 36-41.
Galgano, A. (1992). *Il consulente di direzione come realizzatore*. Milan, Italy: Il Sole 24 Ore.
Gallouj, F. (1984). Les determinants de l'innovation dans les activites de conseil. *Revue Francais du Marketing, Issue 149,* 33-51.
Gammelgaard, J., Husted, K., & Michailova, S. (2005). Knowledge-sharing behaviour and post-acquisition integration failure. In A. F. Buono & F. Poulfelt (Eds.), *Challenges and issues in knowledge management* (pp. 209-226). Greenwich, CT: Information Age Publishing.
Garvin, D. A. (1998). Building a learning organization. In Harvard Business School Press (Ed.), *Harvard Business Review on knowledge management* (pp. 47-80). Boston, Ma: Harvard Business School Press.
Gattiker, U., & Larwood, L. (1985). Why do clients employ management consultants? *Consultation 4*(2), 119-129.
Gelinas, M. V., & James, R. G. (1998). *Collaborative change*. San Francisco, CA: Jossey-Bass/Pfeiffer.
Gelwick, R. (1977). The way of discovery: An introduction to the thought of Michael Polanyi. Oxford, UK: Oxford University Press.
Genova, M., & Montironi, M. (Eds.) (2004). *Knowledge development: Casi e strumenti concreti*. Milan, Italy: FrancoAngeli.

Gephart, M. A., Marsick, V. J., Van Buren, M. E., & Spiro, M. S. (1996). Learning organizations come alive. *Training and Development, 50*(12), 34-46.

Ginsberg, A. (1986). Do external consultants influence strategic adaptation? An empirical investigation. *Consultation, 5*(2), 93-102.

Goldsmith, M. (2006). Where the work of executive coaching lies. *Consulting to Management, 17*(2), 15-17.

Golinelli, G. (2000). *L'approccio sistemico al governo dell'impresa. L'impresa sistema vitale.* Padua, Italy: Cedam.

Goodman, M. A., (2004). *Rasputin for hire: An inside look at management consulting between jobs or as a second career.* Westport, CT: Dialogue Press.

Gore, G. J., & Wright, R. G. (Eds.) (1979). *The academic consultant connection.* New York, NY: Kendall-Hunt.

Gourlay, S. (1999). *Communities of practice: A new concept for the millennium, or the rediscovery of the wheel?* Paper presented at the International Conference on Organizational Learning, Lancaster, UK (June).

Gourlay, S., & Nurse, A. (2005). Flaws in the "engine" of knowledge creation: A critique of Nonaka's Theory. In A. F. Buono & F. Poulfelt (Eds.), *Challenges and issues in knowledge management* (pp. 293-315). Greenwich, CT: Information Age Publishing.

Grant, R. (1996a). Prospering in dynamically-competitive environment: Organizational capability as knowledge integration. *Organization Science, 7*(4), 375-387.

Grant, R. M. (1996b). Toward a knowledge-based theory of the firm. *Strategic Management Journal, 17*(10), 109-122

Grant, R. M., Recchioni, M., & Castello, V. (2004). *Innovazione tecnologica e apprendimento organizzativo.* Rome, Italy: Etas Libri.

Green, H. L. (1963). Management consultants: How to know what you're getting and get what you pay for. *Management Review, 52*(12), 4-16.

Green, C. H. (2006). Create trust, gain a client. *Consulting to Management, 17*(2), 27-29.

Greenbaum, T. L. (1990). *The consultant's manual.* New York, NY: Wiley.
Greenfield, W. M. (1987). *Successful management consulting.* Englewood Cliffs, NJ: Prentice-Hall.
Greenwood, R., & Empson, L. (2003). The professional partnership: Relic or exemplary form of governance? *Organization Studies 24*(6), 909-933.
Greiner, L. E., & Metzger, R. O. (1983). *Consulting to management.* Englewood Cliffs, NJ: Prentice-Hall.
Greiner, L. E., & Nees, G. (1985). Seeing behind the look-alike management consultants. *Organizational Dynamics, 13*(3), 68-79.
Greiner, L., & Poulfelt, F. (Eds.) (2005). *Handbook of management consulting. The contemporary consultant: Insights from world experts.* Mason, Ohio: Thomson South-Western.
Grinstein, G. (1988). A client's eye view of consulting. *Journal of Management Consulting, 4*(2), 3-6.
Groß, C., & Kieser, A. (2006). *Are consultants moving towards professionalization?* In R. Greenwood, R. Suddaby, & M. McDougald (Eds.), *Professional service firms-Research in the Sociology of Organizations-Volume 24* (pp. 69-100). Greenwich, CT: JAI Press.
Gummesson, E. (1978) The marketing of professional services - An organizational dilemma. *European Journal of Marketing 13*(5), 308-318.
Gupta, K. (1997). *A practical guide to needs assessment.* San Francisco, CA: Jossey-Bass/Pfeiffer.
Haas, M. R., & Hansen, M. T. (2005). When using knowledge can hurt performance: The value of organizational capabilities in a management consulting company. *Strategic Management Journal, 26*(1), 1–24.
Hagenmeyer, U. (2007). Integrity in management consulting: A contradiction in terms? *Business Ethics: A European Review, 16*(2), 107-113.
Hagerty, M. R (1997). A powerful tool for diagnosis and strategy. *Journal of Management Consulting, 9*(4), 16-25.
Hall, W. P. (1990). Managing quality in consulting. *Journal of Management Consulting, 6*(3), 44-49.

Hanse, J. J., & Wallgren, L. G. (2007). Job characteristics, motivators and stress among information technology consultants: A structural equation modeling approach. *International Journal of Industrial Ergonomics, 37*(1), 51-59.

Hansen, M. T., Nohria, N., & Tierney T. (1999). What's your strategy for managing knowledge? *Harvard Business Review, 77*(2), 106-116.

Harding, C. F. (1995). Finessing the sale. *Journal of Management Consulting, 8*(4), 53-58.

Harding, F. (1998). *Creating rainmakers: The manager's guide to training professionals.* Holbrook, MA: Adams Media Corps.

Harding, F. (2001). Consultants and salespeople: Mix well before serving. *Consulting to Management, 12*(1), 20-25.

Harding, F. (2002). A better way to cross-sell. *Consulting to Management, 13*(4), 35-38.

Hargadon, A., & Fanelli, A. (2002). Action and possibility: Reconciling dual perspectives of knowledge in organization. *Organization Science, 13*(2), 290-302.

Harris, C. (2001). Consulting and you. *Consulting to Management, 12*(1), 45-52.

Harrison, R. (1995). *Consultant's journey: A dance of work and spirit.* San Francisco, CA: Jossey-Bass.

Hedberg B. (1981). How organizations learn and unlearn. In P. C. Nystrom & W. H. Starbuck (Eds.), *Handbook of Organizational Design - Vol. 1* (pp. 8-27). New York, NY: Oxford University Press.

Hegyi-Gioia, D. M. (1999). Win-win consulting: Ten tips to make your relationship with consultants a success. *Nursing Management, June Issue,* 59-60.

Heller, F. (2002). What next? More critique of consultants, gurus and managers. In T. Clark & R. Fincham (Eds.), *Critical consulting: New perspectives on the management advice industry* (pp. 260-270). Malden. MA: Blackwell Publishers.

Henriksen, L. (2005). In search of knowledge sharing in practice. In A. F. Buono & F. Poulfelt (Eds.), *Challenges and issues in knowledge management* (pp. 155-178). Greenwich, CT: Information Age Publishing.

Herman, R. E. (2006). Expand your thinking. *Consulting to Management, 17*(2), 61-62.

Heusinkveld, S., & Benders, J. (2003). Between professional dedication and corporate design: Exploring forms of new concept development in consultancies. *International Studies of Management & Organization, 32*(4), 104-122.

Heusinkveld, S., & Benders, J. (2005). Contested commodification: Consultancies and their struggle with new concept development. *Human Relations, 58*(3), 283-310.

Holt, M. J. (2006). Learn how you affect your client's bottom line. *Consulting to Management, 17*(2), 60-61.

Holtz, H. (1989). *Choosing and using a consultant.* New York, NY: Wiley.

Holtz, H. (1992). *The consultant's guide to hidden profits.* New York, NY: Wiley.

Holtz, H. (1993). *How to succeed as an independent consultant.* New York, NY: Wiley.

Holtz, H. (1995). *The independent consultant's brochure and letter handbook.* New York, NY: Wiley.

Huczynski, A. (1993). Explaining the succession of management fads. *International Journal of Human Resource Management, 4*(2), 443-463.

Huczynski, A. (1996). *Management gurus: What makes them and how to become one.* London, UK: Routledge.

Ielo, F. (1996). Gli stili di consulenza. *Economia & Management,* Issue 2, 59-66.

Jang, Y., & Lee, J. (1988). Factors influencing the success of management consulting projects. *International Journal of Project Management, 16*(2), 67-72.

Jensen, H. S. (2005). Knowledge and consultancy. In A. F. Buono & F. Poulfelt (Eds.), *Challenges and issues in knowledge management* (pp. 365-375). Greenwich, CT: Information Age Publishing.

Johnson, R. D., Marakas, G. M., & Palmer, J. V. (2000). A theoretical model of differential social attributions toward computing technology: When the metaphor becomes the model. *International Journal of Human Computer Studies, 52*(4), 719-750.

Johnson-Laird, P.N. (1983). *Mental models.* Cambridge, MA: Harvard University Press.

Johnston K., & Withers, J. (1991). *Strategie di successo nei servizi e nella consulenza: Come vendere quello che non si può vedere, gustare, toccare.* Milan, Italy: FrancoAngeli.

Johnston, J. (1963). The productivity of management consultants. *Journal of the Royal Statistical Society, 126*(2), 237- 249.

Kampmeier, C. (1997). High-impact consulting: How clients and consultants can leverage rapid results into long-term gains. *Journal of Management Consulting, 9*(4), 67-68.

Kass, E. E., & Weidner, C. K. (2002). Toward a theory of management consulting: A proposed model and its implications. In A. F. Buono (Ed.), *Developing knowledge and value in management consulting* (pp. 169-207). Greenwich, CT: Information Age Publishing.

Katcher, D. A. (1972). Consulting from within. *California Management Review, 14*(4), 36-44.

Keeble, D., & Schwalbach, J. (1995). *Management consulting in Europe.* Cambridge, MA: ESRC Centre for Business Research.

Kellogg, D. M. (1984). Contrasting successful and unsuccessful OD consultation relationships. *Group & Organization Studies, 9*(2), 151-176.

Kelly, G. A. (1955). *The psychology of personal constructs.* New York, NY: Norton.

Kennedy Information (2007). *Global consulting market place 2007-2010: Key trends, profiles & forecasts.* Peterborough, NH: Kennedy Information.

Kets de Vries, M. F. R. (2006). *The leader on the couch: A clinical approach to changing people and organizations.* San Francisco, CA: Wiley.

Kihn, M. (2005). *House of lies: How management consultants steal your watch and then tell you the time.* New York, NY: Warner Books.

Kilmann, R. H. (1979). Problem defining and the consulting/intervention process. *California Management Review, 21*(3), 26-33.

Kim, D. H. (1993). The link between individual and organizational learning. *Sloan Management Review, 35*(1), 37-50.

Kim, S., & Trimi, S. (2007). IT for KM in the management consulting industry. *Journal of Knowledge Management, 1*(3), 145-155.

Kipping, M. (1996). The US influence on the evolution of management consultancies in Britain, France, and Germany since 1945. *Business and Economic History, 25*(1), 112-123.

Kipping, M. (2001). *Consultancies and the creation of European Management Practice-CEMP Report n. 16.* Uppsala, Sweden: CEMP.

Kipping, M. (2002). Trapped in their wave: The evolution of management consultancies. In T. Clark & R. Fincham (Eds.), *Critical consulting. New perspectives on the management advice industry* (pp. 29-49). Malden, MA.: Blackwell Business.

Kipping, M., & Armbrüster, T. (Eds.) (2000). *The content of consultancy work: Knowledge generation, codification, and dissemination-CEMP Report n. 13.* Uppsala, Sweden: CEMP.

Kipping, M., & Sauviat, C. (1997). *Global management consultancies: Their evolution and structure.* Discussion Papers in International Investment & Business Studies, University of Reading, Department of Economies, Series B, 9(21).

Kirk, J., & Vasconcelos, A. (2003). Management consultancies and technology consultancies in a converging market: A knowledge management perspective. *Electronic Journal of Knowledge Management, 1*(1), 33-46.

Kirsch, L. J., Ko, D. G., & King, W. R. (2005). Antecedents of knowledge transfer from consultants to clients in enterprise system implementations. *MIS Quarterly, 29*(1), 59-85.

Kishel, G., & Kishel, P. (1996). *How to start and run a successful consulting business.* New York, NY: Wiley.

Kogut, B., & Zander, U. (1993). Knowledge of the firm and the evolutionary theory of the multinational corporation. *Journal of International Business Studies, 24*(4), 625-645.

Kolb, D. A., & Frohman, A. L. (1970). An organization development approach to consulting. *Sloan Management Review, 12*(1), 51-65.

Kotler, P., Hayes, T., & Bloom, P. N. (2002). *Marketing professional services: Forward-Thinking strategies for boosting your business, your image, and your profits (2nd ed.).* Paramus, NJ: Prentice-Hall.

Kubr, M. (Ed.) (1993). *How to select and use consultant.* Geneva: Switzerland: International Labour Office.

Kubr, M. (Ed.) (2002.) *Management consulting: A guide to the profession (4th ed.).* Geneva, Switzerland: International Labour Office.

Kumar, V., & Simon, A. (2001). Clients' views on strategic capabilities which lead to management consulting success. *Management Decision, 39*(5), 362-372.

Kumar, V., Simon, A., & Kimberley, N. (2000). Strategic capabilities which lead to management consulting success in Australia. *Management Decision, 38*(1), 24-35.

Labour Research Department (Ed.) (1988). *Management consultants: Who they are and how to deal with them.* London, UK: LRD Publications.

LaGrossa, V., & Saxe, S. (1998). *The consultative approach: Partnering for results!* San Francisco, CA: Jossey-Bass.

Lahti, R., & Beyerlein, M. (2000). Knowledge transfer and management consulting: A look at "the firm". *Business Horizon, 43*(1), 65-74.

Lambert, T. (1997). *High income consulting (2nd ed.).* London, UK: Nicholas Brealey.

Lang, J. C. (2001). Managerial concerns in knowledge management. *Journal of Knowledge Management, 5*(1), 43-57.

Lave, J., & Wenger, E. (1991). *Situated learning: Legitimate peripheral participation.* Cambridge, MA: Cambridge University Press.

Lawrence, C. B. (1999). High value consulting. *Journal of Management Consulting, 10*(3), 76-77.

Leonard, D., & Sensiper, S. (1998). The role of tacit knowledge in group innovation. *California Management Review, 40*(3), 112-132.

Lescarbeau, R., Payette, M., & St-Arnaud, Y. (1990). *Profession consultant.* Paris, France: Editions L'Harmattan.

Lesser, E. L., Fontaine, M. A., & Slusher, J. A. (2000). *Knowledge and communities.* Boston, MA: Butterworth-Heinemann.

Lewin, M. D. (1995). *The overnight consultant.* New York, NY: Wiley.

Linnarsson, H., & Werr, A. (2002). Management consulting for client learning? Clients' perceptions of learning in management consulting. In A. F. Buono (Ed.), *Developing knowledge and value in management consulting* (pp. 3-31). Greenwich, CT: Information Age Publishing.

Lipparini, A. (Ed.) (1998). *Le competenze organizzative: Sviluppo, condivisione, trasferimento.* Rome, Italy: Carocci.

Lipparini, A. (2002). *La gestione strategica del capitale intellettuale e del capitale sociale.* Bologna, Italy: Il Mulino.

Lippitt, G. L., & Lippitt, R. (1986). *The consulting process in action.* San Diego, CA: University Associates.

Lorsch, G. V., & Tierney T. J. (2002). *Aligning the stars: How to succeed when professionals drive success.* Boston; MA: Harvard Business School Press.

Lundberg, C. C., (2002). Consultancy foundations: Toward a general theory. In A. F. Buono (Ed.), *Developing knowledge and value in management consulting* (pp. 153-168). Greenwich, CT: Information Age Publishing.

Macbeth, D. (2002). From research to practice via consultancy and back again: A 14 year case study of applied research. *European Management Journal, 20*(4), 393-400.

Macdonald, S. (2006). From babes and sucklings: Management consultants and novice clients. *European Management Journal, 24*(6), 411-421.

Madigan, C., & O'Shea, J. (1997). *Dangerous company: The consulting powerhouses and the businesses they save and ruin.* New York, NY: Random House (Times Business).

Maister, D. H. (1982). Balancing the professionals service firm. *Sloan Management Review, 24*(1), 15-29.

Maister, D. H. (1984). Industry specialization: Essential but hard to manage. *Journal of Management Consulting, 2*(1), 50-55.

Maister, D. H. (1993). *Managing the professional services firm.* New York, NY: Free Press.

Maister, D. H. (1997). *True professionalism: The courage to care about your people, your clients, and your career.* New York, NY: Free Press.
Maister, D. H. (2001). What drives profits in consulting firms? *Consulting to Management, 12*(2), 45-51.
Maister, D. H., & McKenna, P. J. (2002a). Building team trust. *Consulting to Management, 13*(4), 51-53.
Maister, D. H., & McKenna, P. J. (2002b). *First among equals: How to manage a group of professionals.* New York, NY: Free Press.
March, J. C. (1991). Exploration and exploitation in organizational learning. *Organization Science, 2*(1), 71-87.
Margerison, C. J. (1988). *Managerial consulting skills: A practical guide.* Brookfield, VT: Gower Publishing Company.
Margolis, F. H. (1985). Client-consultant compatibility: The client perspective. In C.R. Bell & L. Nadler (Eds.), *Clients and consultants: Meeting and exceeding expectations* (pp. 118-127). Houston, TX: Gulf Publishing Co.
Marr, B. (2005). Management consulting practice on intellectual capital: Editorial and introduction to special issue. *Journal of Intellectual Capital, 6*(4), 469-473
Martiny, M. (1998). Knowledge management at HP consulting. *Organizational Dynamics, 27*(2), 71-77.
Maturana, H., & Varela F. J. (1987). *The tree of knowledge.* New York, NY: Shambhala.
Maula, M., & Poulfelt, F. (2002). Fit and misfit between codes of conduct and reality in management consulting. *Research in Ethical Issues in Organizations, Volume 4*, 125-143.
McCune, J. C. (1995). The Consultant quandary. *Management Review, 84*(10), 40-43.
McElroy, M. W. (2000). Integrating complexity theory, knowledge management and organizational learning. *Journal of Knowledge Management, 4*(3), 195-203.
McGivern, C. (1983). Some facets of the relationship between consultants and clients in organizations. *Journal of Management Studies, 20*(3), 367-386.
McKenna, C. D. (1995). The origins of modern management consulting. *Business and Economic History, 24*(1), 51-58.

McKenna, C. D. (2006). *The world's newest profession: Management consulting in the twentieth century.* Cambridge, MA: Cambridge University Press.

McLachlin, R. D. (1999). Factors for consulting engagement success. *Management Decision, 37*(5), 394-402.

McNamara, D. (2006). How to build relationships with other professionals. *Consulting to Management, 17*(2), 42-43.

Mercurio, R., & Testa, F. (Eds.) (2000), *Organizzazione, assetto e relazioni nel sistema di business.* Turin, Italy: Giappichelli.

Merron, K. (2005). *Consulting mastery: How the best make the biggest difference.* San Francisco, CA: Berrett-Koehler Publishers.

Merwin, J. (1987). We don't learn from our clients, we learn from each other. *Forbes. Issue 19*(October), 122-128.

Metzger, R. O. (1988). Guidelines for tomorrow's consultants. *Journal of Management Consulting, 4*(4), 13-18.

Michaelson, K. E., & Schaffer, R. H. (1989). The incremental strategy for consulting success. *Journal of Management Consulting, 5*(2), 8-13.

Michaud, C., & Thoenig, J. C. (2004). *Il management cognitivo.* Milan, Italy: FrancoAngeli.

Micklethwait, J., & Wooldridge, A. (1996). *The witch doctors: What the management gurus are saying, why it matters and how to make sense of it.* London, UK: Heinemann.

Miggiani, F. (Ed.) (1994). *Learning organization: Idee e sistemi per lo sviluppo aziendale nella società della conoscenza.* Milan, Italy: Guerini e Associati.

Mills, P. K., & Margulies, N. (1980). Toward a core typology of service organizations. *Academy of Management Review, 5*(2), 255-265.

Minguzzi, P. (2006). *La gestione della conoscenza nelle organizzazioni.* Milan, Italy: FrancoAngeli.

Mitchell, V. W. (1994). Problems and risks in the purchasing of consultancy services. *Service Industries Journal, 14*(3), 315-339.

Mughan, T., Reason, L. L., & Zimmerman, C. (2004). Management consulting and international business support for

SMEs: Need and obstacles. *Education + Training, 46*(8/9), 424-432.

Nachum, L. (1996). Winners and losers in professional service industries: What makes the difference? *Service Industries Journal, 16*(4), 474-490.

Navarro, P. (2006). Help your clients manage the business cycle. *Consulting to Management, 17*(1), 32-34.

Nelson, B., & Economy, P. (1997). *Consulting for dummies.* Foster City, CA: IDG Books.

Nevins, M. D. (1998). Teaching to learn and learning to teach: Notes toward building a university in a management consulting firm. *Career Development International, 3*(5), 185-193.

Newell, S. (2005). The fallacy of simplistic notions of the transfer of "best practice". In A. F. Buono & F. Poulfelt (Eds.), *Challenges and issues in knowledge management* (pp. 51-68). Greenwich, CT: Information Age Publishing.

Nicolai, A. T., & Robken, H. (2005). Scientification, immune responses, and reflection: The changing relationship between management studies and consulting. *Journal of Organizational Change Management, 18*(5), 416-434.

Nonaka, I. (1988). Creating organizational order out of chaos: Self renewal in Japanese firm. *California Management Review, 30*(3), 57-71.

Nonaka, I. (1991). The knowledge-creating company. *Harvard Business Review, 69*, November-December, 96-104.

Nonaka, I. (1994a). A dynamic theory of organizational knowledge-creation. *Organization Science, 5*(1), 14-37.

Nonaka, I. (1994b). Come un'organizzazione crea conoscenza. *Economia e Management*, Issue 3, 31-48.

Nonaka, I. (2000). *Knowledge creation. A source of value.* Houndmills, UK: MacMillan Press.

Nonaka, I., & Takeuchi, H. (1995). *The knowledge-creating company: How Japanese companies create the dynamics of innovation.* New York, NY: Oxford University Press.

Normann, R. (1993). *Service management. Strategy and leadership in service business* (2nd ed.). Chichester, UK: Wiley.

Normann, R. (2001). *Reframing business: When the map changes the landscape.* New York: NY: Wiley.
North, D. C. (2005). *Understanding the process of economic change.* Princeton, NJ: Princeton University Press.
OECD (Ed.) (1999). *The knowledge-based economies: A set of facts and figures.* Paris, France: OECD.
Ormerod, R. J. (1997). The design of organizational intervention: Choosing an approach. *Omega, 25*(4), 415-435.
Ormiston, C. M., & Yoshino, M. Y. (1990). *Bain & Company Inc: Growing the business.* Boston, MA: Harvard Business School Case Services.
Ozley, L. M., & Armenakis, A. A. (2000). "Ethical consulting" does not have to be an oxymoron. *Organizational Dynamics, 28*(4), 38-51.
Panzarani, R. (Ed.) (2004). *Gestione e sviluppo del capitale umano.* Milan, Italy: FrancoAngeli.
Park, D. E. (1990). International reciprocity for consultants. *Journal of Management Consulting, 6*(2), 38-42.
Payne, A. F. T. (1986). New trends in the strategy consulting industry. *Journal of Business Strategy, 7*(1), 43-55.
Payne, A. F. T. (1992). *Marketing and management consulting firms: Towards a relationship marketing approach.* Copenhagen, Sweden: Copenhagen Business School.
Payne, A. F. T. (1993). *Perceptions of management consultants.* Copenhagen, Sweden: Copenhagen Business School.
Payne, A. F. T. (1994). *Developing an international presence: Key issues for management consulting firms.* Copenhagen, Sweden: Copenhagen Business School.
Payne, A. F. T., & Lumsden, C. (1987). Strategy consulting: A shooting star? *Long Range Planning, 20*(3), 53-64.
Pech, R. J., & Mathew, A. (1993). Critical factors for consulting to small business. *Journal of Management Consulting, 7*(3), 61-63.
Penn, R. (1998). The role of consulting knowledge in the transformation of work in contemporary Europe. In J. L. Alvarez (Ed.), *The diffusion and consumption of business knowledge* (pp. 220-228). London, UK: Macmillan Press.

Philips, J. (2006). *How to build a successful consulting practice.* New York, NY: McGraw-Hill.

Phillips, J. (1999). *The Consultant's scorecard: Tracking results and bottom-line impact of consulting projects.* New York, NY: McGraw-Hill.

Pinault, L. (2000). *Consulting demons: Inside the unscrupulous world of global corporate consulting.* New York, NY: Harper Business.

Polanyi, M. (1966). *The tacit dimension.* London, UK: Routledge & Kegan Paul

Polanyi, M. (1985). *Personal knowledge.* Chicago, IL: University of Chicago Press.

Popovich, I. S. (1995). *Managing consultants: How to choose and work with consultants.* Sydney, Australia: Century Business.

Poulfelt, F., Greiner, L., & Bhambri A. (2005). The changing global consulting industry. In L. Greiner & F. Poulfelt (Eds.), *Handbook of management consulting. The contemporary consultant: Insight from world experts* (pp. 3-22). Mason, OH: Thompson South-Western.

Poulfelt, F., & Payne, A. (1994). Management consultants: Client and consultant perspectives. *Scandinavian Journal of Management, 10*(4), 421-436.

Prahalad, C. K., & Hamel, G. (1990). The core competencies of the corporation. *Harvard Business Review, 78*(3), 79-91.

Quagli, A. (2001). *Knowledge management: La gestione della conoscenza aziendale.* Milan, Italy: Egea.

Quinn, J. B. (1992). *Intelligent enterprise: A knowledge and service based paradigm for industry.* New York, NY: MacMillan Press.

Raisel, E. M. (1999). *The McKinsey way.* New York, NY: McGraw-Hill.

Rasiel, E. M., & Friga, P. N. (2002). *The McKinsey mind.* New York, NY: McGraw-Hill.

Rassam, C., & Oates D. (1991). *Management consultancy. The inside story.* London, UK: Mercury Books.

Rawilson, J. G. (1981). *Creative thinking and brainstorming.* Farnborough, Hampshire: Gower.

Reddy, W. B. (1984). *Intervention skills: Process consultation for small groups and teams.* San Francisco, CA: Jossey-Bass.

Reihlen, M., & Ringberg, T. (2006). Computer-mediated knowledge systems in consultancy firms: Do they work? *Research in the Sociology of Organizations, Volume 24,* 307-336.

Reimus, B. (1996). *Knowledge sharing within management consulting firms: Reports on how U.S.-based management consultancies deploy technology, use groupware, and facilitate collaboration.* Fitzwilliam, New Hampshire: Kennedy Publications.

Richards, D. (2006). The human dimension of problem solving. *Consulting to Management, 17*(1), 39-42.

Richter, A., & Niewiem, S. (2004). The changing balance of power in the consulting market. *Business Strategy Review, 15*(1), 8-13.

Rifkin, J. (2000). *L'era dell'accesso.* Milan, Italy: Mondadori.

Riley, R. (1999). Consulting skills as vital as interviewing skills. *Marketing News, 33*(5), 19.

Robertson, M., Scarbrough, H., & Swan, J. (2003). Knowledge creation in professional service firms: Institutional effects. *Organization Studies, 24*(6), 831-857.

Robinson, D. G., & Robinson, J. C. (1996). *Performance consulting: Moving beyond training.* San Francisco, CA: Berrett-Koehler Publishers.

Rosenau Jr, M. D., Sastri, V., & Weiss, A. (2004). Three 2x2 consulting apps. *Consulting to Management, 15*(4), 38-39.

Rossettie, R. (2004). *Secrets of successful consulting.* Bloomington, Indiana: Authorhouse.

Ruef, M. (2002). At the interstices of organizations: The expansion of the management consulting profession, 1933-97. In L. Engwall & K. Sahlin-Andersson (Eds.), *The expansion of management knowledge: Carriers, flows, and sources* (pp. 74-95). Stanford, CA: Stanford University Press.

Ruggles, R. (1998). The state of the notion: Knowledge management in practice. *California Management Review, 40*(3), 80-89.

Rullani, E. (1994). Il valore della conoscenza. *Economia e Politica Industriale,* Issue 82, 47-73.

Rullani, E. (2004a). *Economia della conoscenza. Creatività e valore nel capitalismo delle reti.* Rome, Italy: Carrocci Editore.

Rullani, E. (2004b). *La fabbrica dell'immateriale. Produrre valore con la conoscenza.* Rome, Italy: Carocci Editore.

Rusten, G., Bryson, J. R., & Gammelsaeter, H. (2005) Dislocated versus local business service expertise and knowledge: The acquisition of external management consultancy expertise by small and medium-sized enterprises in Norway. *Geoforum, 36*(4), 525-539.

Rynning, M. (1992). Successful consulting with small and medium-sized vs. large clients: Meeting the needs of the client? *International Small Business Journal, 11*(1), 47-60.

Saint-Onge, H. (1996), Tacit knowledge: The key to the strategic alignment of intellectual capital. *Planning Review, 24*(2), 10-14.

Salvemini, S. (1987). Imprese e consulenza di direzione: Evoluzione di un rapporto. *Finanza, Marketing e Produzione, 1*(2), 45-67.

Sanchez, R. (Ed.) (2001). *Knowledge management and organizational competence.* Oxford, UK: Oxford University Press.

Sanchez, R., & Heene, A. (Eds.) (1997). *Strategic learning and knowledge management.* Chichester, UK: Wiley.

Sarvary, M. (1999). Knowledge management and competition in the consulting industry. *California Management Review, 41*(2), 95-107.

Saxton, T. (1995). The impact of third parties on strategic decision making: Roles, timing and organizational outcomes. *Journal of Organizational Change Management, 8*(3), 47-62.

Scanlan, J. (2006). The Agile Consultant. *Consulting to Management, 17*(2), 22-24.

Scarbrough, H. (2003). The role of intermediary groups in shaping management fashion: The case of knowledge management. *International Studies of Management & Organization, 32*(4), 87-103.

Scarbrough, H., & Swan, J. (2001). Explaining the diffusion of knowledge management. *British Journal of Management, 12*(1), 3-12.

Schaffer, D. N. (1994). Consultants: Is your firm ready for the next wave of office technology? *Journal of Management Consulting, 8*(2), 54-58.

Schaffer, R. H. (1997a). *High-impact consulting: How clients and consultants can leverage rapid results into long-term gains.* San Francisco, CA: Jossey-Bass.

Schaffer, R. H. (1997b). Looking at the 5 fatal flaws of management consulting. *The Journal for Quality and Participation, 20*(3), 44-51.

Schaffer, R. H. (1997c). Beginning with results: The key to success. *The Journal for Quality and Participation, 20*(4), 56-62.

Schaffer, R. H. (1997d). Make consulting pay off: It's time for a new deal. *Industrial Management, 39*(6), 1-6.

Schaffer, R. H. (1998a). Overcome the fatal flaws of consulting: Close the results gap. *Business Horizons, 41*(5), 53-60.

Schaffer, R. H. (1998b). Why pay for recommendations when you need results? *Strategy & Leadership, 26*(3), 34-35.

Schein, E. H. (1987). *Process consultation (Volume 2): Lessons for managers and consultants.* Reading, MA: Addison Wesley.

Schein, E. H. (1988). *Process consultation (Volume 1): Its role in organization development (2nd ed.).* Reading, MA: Addison Wesley.

Schein, E. H. (1999). *Process consultation revisited: Building the helping relationship.* Reading, MA: Addison Wesley.

Schmenner, R. W. (1986). How can services businesses survive and prosper. *Sloan Management Review, 27*(3), 21-32.

Schultz, T. W. (1958). The emerging economic scene and its relation to high school education. In F. S. Chase & H. A. Anderson (Eds.), *The high school in a new era.* Chicago, MA: University of Chicago Press.

Schultz, T. W. (1960). Capital formation by education. *Journal of Political Economy, 68*(12), 571-583.

Schultz, T. W. (1962). Reflections on investment in man. *Journal of Political Economy, 62*(70), 1-8.

Schultz, T. W. (1981). *Investing in people: The economics of population quality.* Berkeley, CA: University of California Press.

Segal, Q. W. (1989). *Evaluation of the Consultancy Initiatives.* London, UK: HMSO.

Semadeni, M. (2001). Toward a theory ok knowledge arbitrage: Examining management consultants as knowledge arbiters and arbitragers. In A. F. Buono (Ed.), *Current trends in management consulting* (pp. 43-67). Greenwich, CT: Information Age Publishing.

Shapiro, E. (1996). *Fad surfing in the boardroom: Managing in the age of instant answers.* Reading, MA: Addison-Wesley.

Shenson, H. L. (1990a). *The contract and fee-setting guide for consultants and professionals.* New York, NY: Wiley.

Shenson, H. L. (1990b). *How to select and manage consultants.* Lexington, MA: Lexington Books.

Shenson, H. L. (1994). *Shenson on consulting.* New York, NY: Wiley.

Shenson, H. L., & Ted, N. (1997). *The complete guide to consulting success: A step-by-step handbook to build a successful consulting practice.* Chicago, MA: Upstart Publishing.

Shenson, H. L., & Wilson, J. R. (1993). *138 quick ideas to get more clients.* New York, NY: Wiley.

Simon, H. (1988). *Le scienze dell'artificiale.* Bologna, Italy: Il Mulino.

Simon, H. (1991). Bounded rationality and organizational learning. *Organization Science*, 2(1), 125-134.

Sivula, P., Van den Bosch, F. A. J., & Elfring, T. (2001). Competence based competition: Gaining knowledge from client relationships. In R. Sanchez (Ed.), *Knowledge management and organizational competence* (pp. 63-76). Oxford, UK: Oxford University Press.

Sorge, C. (2000). *Gestire la conoscenza.* Milan, Italy: Sperling & Kupfer.

Southern, G. (2002). From teaching to practice, via consultancy, and then to research? *European Management Journal*, 20(4), 401-408.

Spender, J. C. (1996). Organizational knowledge, learning and memory: Three concepts in search of a theory. *Journal of Organizational Change*, 9(1), 63-78.

Sperry, L. (1993). Working with executives: Consulting, counseling, and coaching. *Individual Psychology*, 49(2), 257-266.

Steele, F. (1975). *Consulting for organizational change.* Amherst, MA: University of Massachusetts Press.
Stewart, T. A. (1995). Getting real about brainpower. *Fortune,* November 27, 201-203.
Stewart, T. A. (2002). *La ricchezza del sapere: L'organizzazione del capitale intellettuale nel XXI secolo.* Florence, Italy: Ponte alle Grazie.
Stjernberg, T., & Werr, A. (2001). Consulting thought-fully. In B. Hellgren & J. Löwstedt (Eds.), *Managing the thoughtful enterprise* (pp. 259-280). Bergen, Norway: Fagbokforlaget.
Stjernberg, T., & Werr, A. (2003). Exploring management consulting firms as knowledge systems. *Organization Studies,* 24(6), 881-908.
Stroh, K. L., & Johnson, H. H. (2005). *The basic principles of effective consulting.* Mahwah, NJ: Lawrence Erlbaum Associates.
Sturdy, A. (1997). The consultancy process-an insecure business. *Journal of Management Studies,* 34(3), 389-413.
Sturdy, A. (2002). Front-line diffusion: The production and negotiation of knowledge through training interactions. In R. Fincham & T. Clark (Eds.), *Critical consulting: New perspectives on the management advice industry* (pp. 130-151). Malden. MA: Blackwell Publishers.
Szulansky, G. (1996). Exploring internal stickiness: Impediments to the transfer of best practices within the firm. *Strategic Management Journal,* 17(1), 27-43.
TenEyck, R. (1989). Building sound client relationships: One consultant's experience (Part 1). *Journal of Management Consulting* 5(1), 28-32.
Tepper, R. (1993). *The consultant's proposal, fee and contract problem solver.* New York, NY: Wiley.
Testa, F. (1992), *Dall'idea all'impresa: concetti e metodi per lo sviluppo del micro-business.* Padua, Italy: Cedam.
Tierno, D. A., & Young A. (1986). SMR Forum: Growth strategies for consulting in the next decades. *Sloan Management Review,* 27(2), 61-73.
Tilles, S. (1961). Understanding the consultant's role. *Harvard Business Review,* 39(6), 87-99.

Tobin, D. R. (1996). *Transformational learning: Renewing your company through knowledge and skills.* New York, NY: Wiley.

Tobin, D. R. (1998). *The knowledge-enabled organization: Moving from "training" to "learning" to meet business goals.* New York, NY: Amacom.

Todorova, G. (2004). Exploring knowledge issues in the consultant relationship. In A. F. Buono (Ed.), *Creative consulting: Innovative perspectives on management consulting* (pp. 73-98). Greenwich, CT: Information Age Publishing.

Tomassini, M. (1993). *Alla ricerca dell'organizzazione che apprende.* Rome, Italy: Edizioni Lavoro.

Toppin, G., & Czerniawska, F. (2005). *Business consulting: A guide to how it works and how to make it work.* London, UK: Economist.

Turner, A. N. (1982). Consulting is more than giving advice. *Harvard Business Review, 60*(5), 120-128.

Ulvila, J. W., & Brown, R. V. (1982). Decision analysis comes of age. *Harvard Business Review, 60*(5), 130-140.

Vallini, C. (1991). *Fondamenti di governo e direzione d'impresa.* Turin, Italy: Giappichelli.

Van den Bosch, F. A. J. (2003). Management consulting: Emergence and dynamics of a knowledge industry. *Administrative Science Quarterly, 48*(4), 695-699.

Venardos, T. J. (1997). *Consulting success using higher performance standards.* St. Louis, MO: Ness Publishing.

Vicari, S., & Troilo, G. (1999). Creatività organizzativa e generazione di conoscenza: Il contributo della teoria dei sistemi cognitivi. *Sinergie, Issue 50,* 3-24.

Vieira, W. (2006). Whither management consulting? *Consulting to Management, 17*(1), 5-6.

Visscher, K. (2006). Capturing the competence of management consulting work. *Journal of Workplace Learning, 18*(4), 248-260.

Vrakking, W. J. (1989). Consultant's role in technological process innovation. *Journal of Management Consulting, 5*(3), 17-24.

Warglien, M. (1990). *Innovazione e impresa evolutiva: Processi di scoperta e apprendimento in un sistema di routines.* Padua, Italy: Cedam.

Washburn, S. (1995). Coaching the client: Another role for management consultants. *Journal of Management Consulting, 8*(3), 2-3.

Washburn, S. (1996). Challenge and renewal: A historical view of the profession. *Journal of Management Consulting, 9*(2), 47-53.

Weinberg, G. M. (1985). *The secrets of consulting.* New York, NY: Dorset House Publishing.

Weinberg, G. M. (2002). *More secrets of consulting: The consultant's tool kit.* New York, NY: Dorset House Publishing.

Weinshall, T. D. (1982). Help for chief executives: The outside consultant. *California Management Review, 24*(4), 47-58.

Weisbord, M. R. (1987). Toward third-wave managing and consulting. *Organizational Dynamics, 15*(23), 5-24.

Weiss, A. (1992). *Million dollar consulting.* New York, NY: McGraw-Hill.

Weiss, A. (1996). There is less to managing a consulting practice than meets the eye. *Journal of Management Consulting, 9*(1), 14-16.

Weiss, A. (2000a). *Getting started in consulting.* New York, NY: Wiley.

Weiss, A. (2000b). This is not the consulting business anymore? *Consulting to Management, 11*(3), 9-14.

Weiss, A. (2001a). *How to establish a unique brand in the consulting profession.* San Francisco, CA: Jossey-Bass/Pfeiffer.

Weiss, A. (2001b). The majority of "consultants" really ain't. *Consulting to Management, 12*(3), 39-41.

Weiss, A. (2002a). *Great consulting challenges: And how to surmount them.* San Francisco, CA: Jossey-Bass.

Weiss, A. (2002b). *Process consulting: How to launch, implement and conclude successful consulting projects.* New York, NY: Wiley.

Weiss, A. (2003a). *Organizational consulting: How to be an effective change agent.* New York, NY: Wiley.

Weiss, A. (2003b). Solo competencies. *Consulting to Management, 14*(4), 8-10.

Weiss, A. (2003c). That unpleasant image in the mirror. *Consulting to Management, 14*(2), 14-16.

Weiss, A. (2005). *Million dollar consulting toolkit: Step-by-step guidance, checklists, templates, and samples from the million dollar consultant.* Hoboken, NJ: Wiley.

Weiss, A. (2006). Consultant, heal thyself. *Consulting to Management, 17*(2), 10-12.

Wells, R., G. (1983). What every manager should know about management consultants. *Personnel Journal, 62*(2), 142-148.

Werr, A. (2002). The internal creation of consulting knowledge: A question of structuring experience. In L. Engwall & M. Kipping (Eds.), *Management consulting: Emergence and dynamics of a knowledge industry* (pp.92-108). Oxford, UK: Oxford University Press.

Werr, A., & Styhre, A. (2003). Management consultants-Friend or foe? Understanding the ambiguous client-consultant relationship. *International Studies of Management & Organization, 32*(4), 43-66.

Whittle, A. (2006). The paradoxical repertoires of management consultancy. *Journal of Organizational Change Management, 19*(4), 424-436.

Wickham, P. A. (1999). *Management consulting.* London, UK: Pitman Publishing.

Wiig, K. M. (1993). *Knowledge management foundations. Thinking about thinking: How organizations create, represent and use knowledge.* Arlington, TX: Schema Press.

Williams, R. (2004). Management fashions and fads: Understanding the role of the consultants and managers in the evolution of ideas. *Management Decision, 42*(6), 769-780.

Wright, C., & Kitay, J. (2002). But does it work? Perceptions of the impact of management consulting. *Strategic Change, 11*(5), 271-278.

Zamarian, M. (2002). *Le routine organizzative: Percorsi di apprendimento e riproduzione.* Turin, Italy: Utet.